Biking the GRAND CANYON *Area*

TEXT AND PHOTOGRAPHY BY
ANDREA LANKFORD

WESTCLIFFE PUBLISHERS
westcliffepublishers.com

International Standard Book Number: 1-56579-479-6

Text and photography copyright: Andrea Lankford, 2003. All rights reserved.

Editor: Jenna Samelson Browning
Designer: Carol Pando
Production Manager: Craig Keyzer

Published by:
Westcliffe Publishers, Inc.
P.O. Box 1261
Englewood, CO 80150
westcliffepublishers.com

Printed in the USA by: Versa Press, Inc.

Library of Congress Cataloging-in-Publication Data:
Lankford, Andrea.
    Biking the Grand Canyon area / text and photography by Andrea Lankford.
       p. cm.
    Includes bibliographical references (p.) and index.
    ISBN 1-56579-479-6
      1. All terrain cycling--Arizona--Grand Canyon--Guidebooks. 2. Grand Canyon
(Ariz.)--Guidebooks. I. Title.
GV1045.5.A62G735 2003
796.6'3'0978865--dc21   2003049713

For more information about other fine books and calendars from Westcliffe Publishers, please contact your local bookstore, call us at 1-800-523-3692, write for our free color catalog, or visit us on the Web at westcliffepublishers.com.

Please Note: Risk is always a factor in backcountry travel. Many of the activities described in this book can be dangerous, especially when weather is adverse or unpredictable, and when unforeseen events or conditions create a hazardous situation. The author has done her best to provide the reader with accurate information about backcountry travel, as well as to point out some of its potential hazards. It is the responsibility of the users of this guide to learn the necessary skills for safe backcountry travel, and to exercise caution in potentially hazardous areas. The author and publisher disclaim any liability for injury or other damage caused by backcountry traveling or performing any other activity described in this book.

Front Cover: *The views at Point Sublime (Ride 17) live up to its name.*
Previous Page: *Ride 27, Jumpup Point*

Acknowledgments

I am indebted to all those who gave me advice and information, who provided a couch or bed for me to sleep on and a shower for me to clean up in, who patiently modeled for the photographer, who generously fed the hungry writer, or who otherwise helped with this project: Bryan and Cale Wisher; Mike McGinnis; A.J. Legault; Melanie, Jackson, and Luke Pergiel; Mary, Scott, Tyler, and Jerra Hinson; Beth and Dan Overton; and Jack Welch (Coconino Cycling Club).

My gratitude extends to all the friendly folks at the Jacob Lake Visitor Center (USFS and NPS), who were always helpful whenever I called or stopped by with "just one more question." I especially thank Kim Besom (NPS), who found the exciting historic photographs of bicyclists at the Grand Canyon, designed the petroglyph-style biking graphic that highlights the family rides, and continues to be encouraging and helpful in so many other ways.

I also want to thank Linda Doyle at Westcliffe Publishers, Daniel D'Ambrosio of *Adventure Cyclist* magazine, and Laura Clymer of the *Arizona Daily Sun* for taking a chance on me when I was an infant writer. This is a much better book because of the diligence of editor Jenna Browning.

Thanks to "my favorite thing," Kent Delbon, for being the best husband in the world.

Most of all, thanks to my mother, Patricia Lankford, for supporting me and encouraging me to write this book.

This book is dedicated to the memory of Cale Shaffer (1974–2000), a Grand Canyon park ranger who gave his life for the cause.

Photo by Brittney Ruland

Cale Shaffer at Indian Garden Ranger Station.

Contents

Ride 14, Coconino Rim Loop

Foreword

Every year, increasing numbers of people visit the Grand Canyon area. Many motorists find themselves fighting traffic in the search for a parking spot during high season. Along with heightened visitation, the quest for unique ways to enjoy the canyon also grows. *Biking the Grand Canyon Area* offers visitors the opportunity to experience the canyon from a fresh perspective while helping to minimize park traffic problems by traveling by bicycle.

At Grand Canyon National Park, the National Park Service supports efforts to reduce traffic congestion by encouraging visitors to use alternative modes of transportation. Bike travel provides ease of movement through the park, as well as access to some of its most peaceful places. The ongoing development of the Greenway and village bike paths will allow bicyclists to move efficiently in and around the developed areas on both rims of the Grand Canyon. For those looking for more challenge, the park's fire roads provide intermediate riders access to remote trailheads, and the Kaibab National Forest adjacent to the park has trails built specifically for mountain bikers.

When Andrea (Andy) Lankford asked me to share my thoughts on biking at the Grand Canyon, I thought back to the times I had biked

The best way to immerse yourself in a North Rim biking experience is to take a vehicle-supported camping trip.

on the South Rim. My first assignment at the Grand Canyon was as a patrol ranger in the late 1980s. I often pedaled the park fire roads as part of my physical fitness training. On the weekends, I biked the longer routes to get away from the crowds and to clear my head after grueling workweeks during the peak of the summer season. Now that I am chief ranger and the father of two young boys, my bike rides are slower-paced, family-oriented explorations that focus less on physical exertion. We seem to spend more time off our bikes looking at bugs than we do going anywhere. Whatever your style, Andy has described a trip that will work for you.

Andy Lankford and I first got to know each other when we were rangers at Yosemite National Park. The volume and intensity of the emergency response workload in parks like Yosemite and the Grand Canyon make many rangers hesitate to sign up to work in such pressure-cooker environments. When new rangers do show up, the other rangers immediately size them up to see who will make the cut. I clearly remember Andy on her first day of work. With her laid-back, easygoing manner and Southern drawl, at first, Andy seemed out of place. But after we had worked a few "adventures in rangering" incidents together, I quickly learned not to underestimate her. Andy isn't easily intimidated. Her tenacity is legendary among her friends.

Andy's tenacity shows in this thoroughly researched, well-written guide. Most important, it was penned by someone who understands what she is talking about. Andy spent days pedaling around the North and South Rims with friends and their families. She combines her knowledge of long-distance biking and hiking with her training as a Grand Canyon ranger, giving readers insider tips on how to best prepare for a Grand Canyon biking adventure. Andy's firsthand experience makes *Biking the Grand Canyon Area* a valuable guide for bicyclists of all levels who want to ride in the grandest of locations.

—Chris Pergiel
Chief Ranger, Grand Canyon National Park

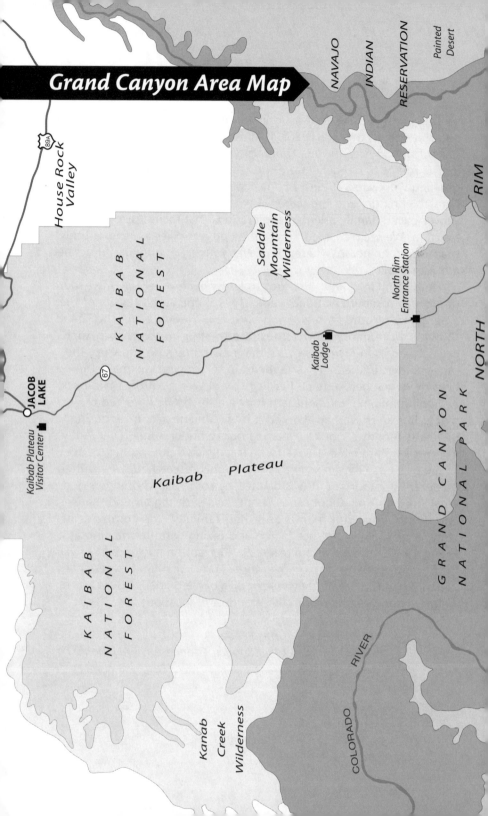

Grand Canyon Area Map

NAVAJO INDIAN RESERVATION

Painted Desert

RIM

House Rock Valley

Saddle Mountain Wilderness

North Rim Entrance Station

KAIBAB NATIONAL FOREST

NORTH

Kaibab Lodge

JACOB LAKE

Kaibab Plateau Visitor Center

Kaibab Plateau

GRAND CANYON NATIONAL PARK

KAIBAB NATIONAL FOREST

COLORADO RIVER

Kanab Creek Wilderness

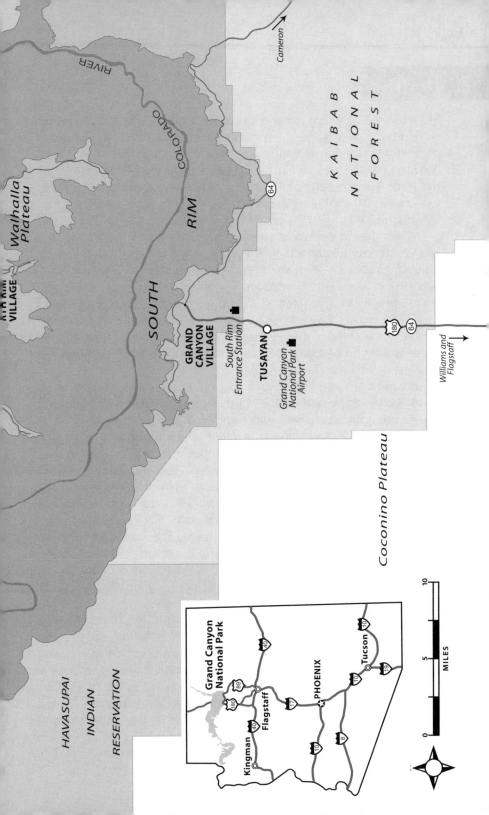

Preface

I had my first bicycling experiences at the Grand Canyon while I was working as a park ranger on the South Rim from 1995 to 1999. For park rangers, the hectic South Rim can involve long days of working hard to keep the park safe from the people and the people safe from the park. On weekends and afternoons, I would get away from the crowds by exploring the dirt roads and Forest Service trails by mountain bike.

What I found cheered a summer-frazzled park ranger's heart: well-built mountain bike trails with more elk prints than tire tracks; quiet dirt roads through shady forests of ponderosa pine; paved paths for easy access to overlooks, visitor centers, grocery stores, gift shops, and restaurants. Most of the time, I had these bike trails all to myself. I imagined that some of the easier paths would be perfect for families. It seemed a shame that more people didn't know about these wonderful biking options centered around one of the world's greatest natural wonders.

It wasn't until the fall of 2000 that I discovered the amazing biking opportunities to be had on the North Rim. A friend and I had come down with a peculiar illness that compelled us to become the first to mountain bike 800 miles along the length of the Arizona Trail from Utah to Mexico. While I negotiated the winding Arizona Trail through the alpine scenery of the Kaibab Plateau, what I saw stunned me. I knew I had to come back to see more of what the North Rim had to offer.

While researching this book, I found rides, like the Rainbow Rim Trail, that mountain bikers had been using for years. But I also found rides that, until now, were seemingly undiscovered. The North Rim trips I've described in these pages include plenty of opportunities for meadow-rolling, wildlife-spotting, rim-skirting, sunset-watching, overlook-gazing fun. But don't just take my word for it. Go see for yourself. The Kaibab Plateau is a nature-lover's mountain biking paradise.

An exciting future lies ahead for bicycling at the Grand Canyon. The National Park Service has already begun the complex and tedious process of planning and building a multi-use greenway along the South Rim to Desert View. This book describes the first completed sections of the greenway system, which one day might make the Grand Canyon one of the best bicycling parks in the nation. But you don't have to wait until then. Right now, paved cycling trails on the South Rim give families and beginners a chance to join the biking fun. I designed *Biking the Grand Canyon Area* with all levels of mountain bikers in mind. I've even included a few routes that work for road cyclists. Whether you intend to haul your 2-year-old behind you in a trailer or you want to jump a few logs and lean into some tight turns, you'll find what you are looking for in this book.

So, what are you doing just standing there? Grab a bike and get rolling! But before you go, I'd like to leave you with the words of my friend and former Grand Canyon park ranger, Cale Shaffer: "May the canyon colors bring smiles to your faces."

—Andrea Lankford

Bike Trails provide a scenic way to escape the Grand Canyon's Crowds.

Introduction

ABOUT THE GRAND CANYON

Geography

For the practical purposes of this book, the Grand Canyon is divided into three geographical areas, the North Rim, the South Rim, and the Inner Canyon. The Inner Canyon, the big space that makes the Grand Canyon famous, consists of the area below the rims. This area is closed to bicycles. The extreme terrain of the Inner Canyon makes this area unridable for the most part, anyway.

The area appropriate for mountain biking is the relatively flat terrain on the North and South Rims of the Grand Canyon. The Inner Canyon divides a broad plateau into two parts, with approximately 277 miles of "rim" on each side. On the north side lies the Kaibab (Ky-bab) Plateau, and on the south side, the Coconino (Co-co-nee-no) Plateau. With elevations ranging from 6,500 to 9,100 feet, the North Rim/Kaibab Plateau offers alpine scenery and cool temperatures even during the summer. In winter, it receives an average of 128 inches of snow. The elevations found on the South Rim/Coconino Plateau, on the other hand, are between 5,000 and 7,500 feet. South Rim daytime summer temperatures can approach highs of 90 degrees Fahrenheit, but nights are relatively cool. Although the North Rim becomes snowed-in most winters, the South Rim receives, on average, only half as much snow.

Geology

Whoa. Don't fall asleep yet. The impressive result of millions of years of geologic forces at work on the Grand Canyon is the biggest reason you go there, so a little painless geology lesson should be in order. Know The Canyon's History. Study Rocks Made By Time. That's the acronym taught to new park rangers so they can learn the names of the Grand Canyon's geologic layers. During your trip, you can find the names to fit the acronym by checking out the exhibits at Yavapai Point, the Canyon View Information Plaza, and other overlooks, but I will tell you that the **K** is for Kaibab limestone. At more than 200 million years old, the Kaibab Formation is the canyon's youngest geologic layer—the layer that your bike tires will be on while you travel on the North and South Rims. If you look carefully, you might discover signs of the abundant fossils that are found in this formation.

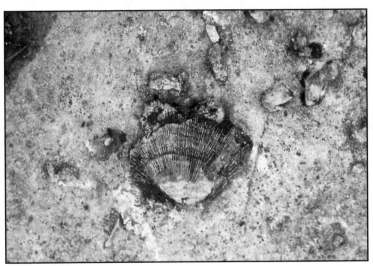

Kaibab limestone often contains fossils.

Hint: Look for stripes that resemble the back of a seashell pressed into the rock. If you find something that looks a little like the symbol on Shell service station signs, you are seeing a brachiopod (above)—evidence of the time when a vast sea covered this area.

For a quick and dirty explanation of how the canyon was formed, imagine the layers of the Grand Canyon as a cake and the Colorado River as a knife. Someone pushes up on the cake while someone else cuts down and back with the knife. The cut left behind in the cake is the Grand Canyon. As geologic forces uplifted the Kaibab and Coconino Plateaus, the Colorado River simultaneously and slowly cut down through the layers of the Grand Canyon. Of course, the full explanation is much more complicated than the cake scenario, and even geologists cannot completely explain how the canyon was formed. Some visitors choose to simply enjoy the scenery and leave the science to the scientists, but if this analogy has whetted your appetite for Grand Canyon geology, see Appendix D for several recommended books on the subject.

Habitat Zones of the North and South Rims

Mountain Grassland Parks (North Rim only): 8,000 to 9,100 feet

These are the wonderful alpine meadow basins and shallow valleys that make the North Rim trails such a pleasure to ride. Be on the lookout for wild turkeys in the morning and coyotes in the evening. Expect spectacular wildflower displays in the summer months, especially after wet winters. Scientists have several theories about why these meadows exist. Snowmelt might cause overly wet conditions that prohibit tree seedlings from taking root, or natural soil toxins might allow the growth of grasses but inhibit the encroachment of trees. No one knows for sure. Either way, the meadows of the North Rim remain a pleasant mystery.

Boreal Forest (North Rim only): 8,000 to 9,100 feet

The spruce-fir forests on the North Rim resemble the environments you would find if you traveled to Canada. The explosive wing beats of a blue grouse might give you a shock when you spook this bird out of the brush, and prepare to be scolded by red squirrels (or chickarees) chattering at you from the safety of tree branches. In late September, the aspen put on a dramatic show with their shimmering gold leaves.

Ponderosa Pine Forest (both rims): 7,000 to 8,250 feet

An open, parklike atmosphere characterizes the stately ponderosa forest. Elk sightings occur here frequently during the warmer months. In

summer, look for the purple blooms of lupine on the pine needle–covered forest floor. The ponderosa forest is home to the Kaibab squirrel on the North Rim and Abert squirrel on the South Rim. Separated for centuries by the genetic barrier we call the Grand Canyon, these squirrels have evolved into two different subspecies. On the North Rim, the Kaibab squirrel has a dark, almost black, body that contrasts starkly with its white,

Abert squirrel, circa 1930s. Courtesy Grand Canyon National Park, image #GRCA 31629.

bushy tail and ear tufts. On the South Rim, the Abert squirrel sports a reddish-gray coat and only the underside of its tail is white.

Piñon-Juniper Woodland (both rims): 4,000 to 7,000 feet

When winter's frigid air hits the higher elevations, the elk herds descend to the piñon-juniper woodlands, or what some people call the "P-J" forest. The Utah juniper and the piñon pine are the dominant plants in this life zone. Mule deer, piñon jays, and the common raven are among the wildlife species often seen here. The piñon-juniper woodland receives between 10 and 20 inches of precipitation each year. The harsher growing conditions near the edge of the canyon often stunt the trees there, lending them a twisted appearance resembling bonsai trees.

History of Bicycling at the Grand Canyon

With progress being made toward the construction of more than 45 miles of greenway trails on the South Rim and perhaps 28 miles of multipurpose trails on the North Rim, bicycling at the Grand Canyon has an exciting future. However, many do not realize that Grand Canyon bicycling also has an intriguing past.

More than a century ago, before the Grand Canyon was even a national park, the *Coconino Sun* printed reports of "wheelmen" exploring the South Rim of the Grand Canyon by "wheel." In 1895, the Flagstaff

Long-distance cyclists. Photo by Emery Kolb, circa 1928.
Courtesy Grand Canyon National Park, image #6843.

American Youth Hostel group at Grand Canyon Depot, 1947. Photo by Virgil Gipson. Courtesy Grand Canyon National Park, image #998.

newspaper reported that J.C. Vining, "an expert bicyclist," toured the Grand Canyon by bicycle. In January 1896, a group of biking enthusiasts created the Coconino Cycling Club. The Flagstaff-based club planned annual "runs" to the Grand Canyon along what is now known as the Moqui Stagecoach Route.

From 1892 to 1901, when the railroad was completed, the Grand Canyon–Flagstaff Stagecoach transported people and supplies to the Grand Canyon. The trip took all day and stopped at three staging areas along the way so passengers and horses could rest before continuing the dusty, kidney-busting ride. Back then, "wheelmen" rode single-speed bicycles along the 80-mile route; some completed the trip in eight hours, which was faster than the six-horse stagecoach. The tradition of bicycling between Flagstaff and the Grand Canyon along the stage line continues today when members of the Coconino Cycling Club bike the entire route almost every fall. For more information on the history of the stagecoach line, read *Grand Canyon–Flagstaff Stage Coach Line: A History & Exploration Guide* by Richard K. and Sherry G. Mangum.

My favorite "wheelman" traveled the route in August 1897. According to the August 26, 1897 edition of the *Coconino Sun*, Edith Brooks of Phoenix became the first woman to complete the ride from Flagstaff to the Grand Canyon. The paper reported that she made the trip with "comparative ease and was frequently compelled to slow up in her speed to allow the wagon to catch up." It seems as if the editors were concerned that some readers might assume that, because a female had accomplished the Grand Canyon run, the route was less than challenging. So they added this comment: "The ride to the Grand Canyon is in reality a trip that taxes the endurance of our best male bicyclists on account of the grade encountered." In October 2000, my friend Beth Overton and I followed the tire tracks of Edith Brooks when we became the first *people* to mountain bike the 800-mile length of the Arizona Trail, 80 miles of which are along the Moqui Stagecoach Route. Unlike Edith, however, Beth and I benefited from luxuries such as suspension forks, granny gears, and sports bras.

I have to take my helmet off to the two men in a 1928 photograph taken by one of the Kolb brothers, famous early photographers of the Grand Canyon. Wearing sailor uniforms and posing on the rim with their bicycles, these two young men stopped at the Grand Canyon while on a long-distance cycling trip from Los Angeles to New York (see p. 15). From the photograph, it appears that the men had chained themselves to their bicycles, no doubt to ensure that the long miles did not weaken their dedication. The National Park Service photograph archives also have a photo from 1947 that shows a perky group of 14 young men and women from the American Youth Hostel posing with their bikes in front of the Grand Canyon Depot (opposite). It is nice to think that, with the Greenway, the bicycling tradition at the Grand Canyon will continue well into the new millennium.

BIKING IN THE GRAND CANYON AREA

Hazards

If you take the proper precautions, biking on the rims of the Grand Canyon is a relatively safe activity. However, during my 12-year career as a Search and Rescue Ranger and Wilderness EMT for the National Park Service, I saw firsthand how improper planning, poor decision-making, unpreparedness, and foolish behavior can turn a fun vacation into a tragic nightmare. Please pay attention to all the warnings mentioned in this book and posted on trailhead signs. Bike smart. Bike safe.

For a fascinating and informative read about the many fatal mishaps that have occurred at the Grand Canyon, pick up *Over the Edge: Death in Grand Canyon* by Michael P. Ghiglieri and Thomas M. Myers. Although the topic is morbid, the lessons you can learn from this book can help you avoid the mistakes others have made. This book also gives you an idea of the type of occupational hazards and frustrations Grand Canyon park rangers face almost daily.

Hypothermia

On the North Rim, at 6,000 to 9,100 feet, you must be prepared for weather extremes. You might want to carry a few hand warmers and plastic bags. If you or someone in your group gets wet and cold or begins to shiver uncontrollably, and you cannot get to shelter, remove his or her wet clothes and use the plastic bags as vapor barriers to hold in warmth. Have him or her eat high-calorie foods and drink warm liquids.

High-Altitude Sickness

If you live at a low elevation, you will have to take time to acclimate to the lower oxygen levels present at higher elevations. Some people experience symptoms of high-altitude sickness at elevations as low as 6,000 feet. Headache, dizziness, nausea, and difficulty breathing are some of the more common symptoms. If you think you or a member of your group is suffering from high-altitude sickness, descend to a lower elevation as soon as possible.

Heat Illnesses

Dehydration, heat exhaustion, and heat stroke can be difficult to distinguish from one another. Symptoms such as nausea, an altered mental state, fatigue, and hot/dry or cool/moist skin can occur in all three conditions. If you suffer from high blood pressure or similar conditions, or take medications to treat such conditions, contact your doctor for advice before exposing yourself to the risk of heat-related illnesses.

Heat illnesses are a huge problem in the Inner Canyon, but cooler temperatures at the rims' higher elevations minimize the risk of developing such conditions there. Still, it is important to stay properly hydrated. Rescue rangers at the Grand Canyon recommend that you monitor your urine output to keep track of your hydration level. Dark yellow or brown urine might mean you are dehydrated. Clear urine usually indicates you are well hydrated. Maintaining your urine at a pale yellow color is optimum.

While it's important to stay hydrated, a condition called hypo-natremia— low brain and blood sodium—can arise if you drink excessive amounts of water, sweat out too much salt, and don't replace lost electrolytes by eating adequately. Cramping muscles can also result from low electrolyte levels in the muscles. Eating salty and high-carbohydrate foods can help balance electrolyte levels.

If you decide to take a hike down into the canyon during your trip, be sure to read the hiker safety information posted at most trailheads and visitor centers before you start. You can prevent heat exhaustion and heat stroke by avoiding exertion during the hottest part of the day. Ride or hike during the early morning or late afternoon. If heat levels are high, get into the shade before you start to feel uncomfortable. If water is plentiful, wet down shirts, hats, and bandannas to enhance your body's evaporative-cooling abilities.

Should a member of your group begin to act strangely or become unconscious, that person might be experiencing heat stroke, a life-threatening condition caused by extremely high body temperatures. Move the victim out of the sun and wet him or her down, or, if possible, submerge him or her in cool water, to lower the body temperature.

Lightning

Several people were struck by lightning during the time I worked as a ranger at the Grand Canyon. The high points along the rim are especially prone to receiving lightning strikes. During the summer monsoon season (late June to mid-September), plan on avoiding open spaces near the rim, ridgelines, and other prominent exposed areas during the afternoons. If you are caught in a lightning storm, stay away from lone trees or rocks and avoid shallow caves or depressions, as these areas might attract arcs of electricity. Put a foam pad, clothing, or some other form of insulation between yourself and the ground, then squat or sit in a balled-up position, hugging your knees to your chest.

Wildlife

Mountain lions are frequently seen at the Grand Canyon. The chance of being attacked by one is extremely remote, especially if you travel in a group. If you do encounter a mountain lion that seems aggressive, stand your ground, make yourself look big by picking up your bike, speak firmly, and otherwise give the impression that "I'm a predator just like you, so back off." If attacked, fight back!

Vegetation

Prickly pear cactus, yucca, and agave are a few of the spiny plants that you might encounter if you ride off the paved trails. Getting your bike tires treated with a thorn-resistant fluid can be well worth the minimal cost. Ask your local bike shop for more information.

The spiny banana yucca awaits unsuspecting bike tires.

Getting Lost

Even with maps and a guidebook, you can get lost in the maze of ponderosa and piñon-juniper woodlands if you get off track while riding in remote national forest areas. Stay alert and have at least one member of your group who is comfortable interpreting maps. Day riders heading into remote areas should carry a jacket, food and water, a flashlight, and other gear to get them through an emergency overnight stay in the backcountry. When traveling in a group, make a rule that the lead cyclist will always wait at any fork or turn that has even a remote possibility of being confusing. This way, your group won't get separated.

Aches and Pains

In my experience, traveling by bike is much easier on your body than hiking or jogging. Blisters are usually not an issue. Soreness is rare and less severe. Recovery is quicker. However, knee strain and chafing are common biker ailments that can spoil a trip. Refer to Appendix D for a list of books that give detailed information on injuries and strains common to bicycling and backcountry travel.

Hints: Bring a tube of chamois butter to prevent and soothe chafing. Make sure your bike seat is adjusted properly to prevent knee strain. Don't overdo it: Increase your skill and fitness levels gradually.

Crashes

Helmet. Helmet. Helmet. Wear your helmet at all times when you are in motion on your bike, and make sure it fits snugly. If the terrain is above your skill level, dismount and walk your bike. Riding through intimidating sections just to say you did it is not worth having to end your trip because of injury. Wear gloves to protect your hands in case you fall. Wear protective eyewear or sunglasses while riding. While on roadways open to motorized use, ride with the direction of traffic and obey all traffic laws. Wear bright clothing and avoid riding during low-light times of the day.

Hunting Season

During the fall in the national forest areas on both the North and South Rims, you will most likely encounter hunters. They will be friendly, but it is a good idea to wear bright clothing so they can see you more easily.

Mind Your Manners

Bike enthusiasts are fortunate that the National Park Service has been progressive in including bicycling as a recreational option in the management plan for Grand Canyon National Park. However, there are still some concerns that mountain bikers do not respect park rules and regulations and cause damage to the park's natural resources. During your Grand Canyon bicycling trip, please help to ensure the future of biking in our national parks by being polite, environmentally conscious, law-abiding, low-impact users of the backcountry.

Minimize Your Impact on the Environment

• Stay on established trails and roads.

• Stay off trails and out of other areas that are closed to bicycles. Do not take your bicycle into official Wilderness Areas. Apart from those listed in this book, most trails in the national park are closed to bicycles unless posted or otherwise designated.

• Camp in designated or previously impacted campsites whenever possible. Camp at least 100 yards from natural water sources.

• Use the provided restroom facilities, or, if none are to be found, go a good distance (at least 100 yards) from campsites and trails to do your business. Bury human waste in a "cathole" at least 6 inches deep. Make sure you are at least 100 yards away from water sources.

Ideal campsites like this one on the North Rim abound in the Kaibab National Forest

• Rarely build campfires. Use preexisting fire rings and always put out your fire with water until the coals are cold to touch. Use a stove for cooking.

• Pack out all trash. This includes pieces of the wrappers from sports bars and gels, cigarette butts, fruit peels, toilet paper, and feminine-hygiene products.

• Do not feed the wildlife. Feeding the deer attracts them to the roads, where they are more likely to get hit by cars. Junk food is not appropriate for the digestive systems of wild animals.

Minimize Your Impact on Other Users

• Give hikers the right-of-way. Slow down or stop and be sociable. Smile and say hello. Thank them if they step aside to let you pass. Share some of the experiences you have had or the sights you have seen.

• Give equestrians the right-of-way. The sight of a mountain bike might spook some horses. Stop a good distance before you reach the horse and rider. Say hello to the rider and ask him or her what you should do. When in doubt, get off your bike and let the horse pass safely.

• Respect the wishes of private landowners. Follow the directions of any posted signs. Ask permission before camping or using water sources on private property.

• Leave gates in the position you found them.

• Obey the rules and regulations of the areas you travel through.

• Stay alert. Report suspicious activity to the appropriate authorities.

• Respect historic and archaeological sites. Avoid camping near archaeological sites and leave them as you found them.

• Save taxpayers some money. Don't put search and rescue workers at risk by getting hurt or lost, or requesting help when it is not necessary. Use good judgment. Bike smart. Make avoiding injury more important than finishing your trip or logging miles. Be prepared for emergencies. If someone in your group is injured or ill, attempt to self-rescue when possible and when it won't aggravate the situation. Use common sense.

• Volunteer. Join a trail association in your area and take part in its trail-maintenance projects.

PLANNING YOUR TRIP

When to Go

South Rim: All Year

You can ride many of the trails on the South Rim year-round. If you go during the fall or spring, you have a better chance of avoiding the crowds. During the summer, the South Rim is mostly pleasant with occasional highs in the 90s. Winter can be chilly, but during dry winters, most of these trails should be ridable. During wet winters, however, you might run into weather that leaves the South Rim covered with snow for several days. The National Park Service plows the paved paths, so you can ride the paved trails and roads even when snow covers the rest of the ground.

North Rim: Mid-June to Mid-October

The best months for mountain bikers to visit the North Rim are July, August, and September. Sometimes after wet winters, snow might linger on the North Rim until late June. In addition, snowmelt might make the trails muddy until later in the summer. Fall temperatures can be quite chilly at night, but the stunning fall colors should make up for it.

Choosing a Bike

For riding on pavement, any bike will do. For riding the trails, especially on the North Rim, I recommend a mountain bike with a front-suspension fork to ease the jarring on your arms and hands as you bounce over bumpy roads and trails. At the time of this printing, there are no bike shops at or near the Grand Canyon, so be sure your bike is in top working condition before you get there and carry the equipment listed in the following section. Future NPS plans include the construction of a bike rental facility near the Canyon View Information Plaza, but for now, see Appendix B for a list of companies near the Grand Canyon that rent bikes.

Bike Equipment, Repair, and Maintenance

The bike-repair shops closest to the South Rim are in Flagstaff, Arizona, and those most convenient to the North Rim are in St. George, Utah. See Appendix B for a list of shops. The best ways to avoid equipment problems are to carry the items recommended in this section and to educate yourself on how to make bike repairs in the field. You'll find several recommended books on the subject in Appendix D.

Tires

It is a good idea to carry at least one spare inner tube, pump, and patch kit per person whenever you are traveling more than a few miles. Have your tires treated with a puncture-resistant sealant before you ride.

Gloves

Bicycling gloves pad the shock from bumps and protect your hands in case of a fall. Padded full-fingered gloves will give you the best protection. Waterproof gloves are nice in cold and rainy weather.

Helmet

Don't ride without it. Make sure it fits snugly.

Bicycle Odometer (Cyclometer)

Highly recommended, especially on remote routes, as an aid to route finding.

Tools

Compact multitool kits have most of the tools you will need for routine field repairs. Here is a list of tools that I suggest you have with you or in your support vehicle during an extended bike trip.

- Set of Allen wrenches
- Small rag
- Small Phillips-head and flathead screwdrivers
- Bottle of chain lubricant
- Chain tool and spare links
- Duct and electrical tape
- Small adjustable wrench
- Length of multipurpose cord
- Three plastic tire levers
- Spare cleat (if applicable)
- Spare inner tube
- Patch kit
- Spare tire for group (self-sealing or puncture-resistant tubes)
- Spoke wrench and spare spokes
- Spare bolts (for seat post, rack, shoe cleats, toe clips, etc.)
- Spare brake pads
- Travel-size emergency bike-repair manual and/or a good knowledge of how to use all these tools

Water Bottles or Hydration Backpacks

It is a good idea to have at least one water bottle for each bike, even when on short rides. Fanny packs and hydration backpacks are handy for carrying a few snacks, money, and other gear as well as water.

Riding with Children

There are several methods for carrying younger children who are not ready to ride their own bikes. Most of the information I found recommended that you wait until your child is one year or older before taking him or her with you on your bike. There is concern that babies cannot handle the bumps that come with bicycling. According to the League of American Bicyclists, a good rule of thumb is that your child needs to be able to hold his or her head up and needs to have a head big enough to fit into a helmet before going biking with you. (The head should fit into the helmet with minimal padding and the straps should fit snugly under the child's chin.) If you have any doubt, please ask your pediatrician for advice. I've listed a few books in Appendix D for parents who want more advice on bicycling with children.

When it comes to biking safety, good habits start early.

If your child is ready to accompany you, be sure to try out the gear before you put your child in it and before you leave home. Most of the rides listed in this book are in areas where vehicle traffic is light or non-existent, but please use a helmet and other safety gear appropriate for your child every time you ride. Check your local outdoor retailer or visit www.rei.com for the following child carriers, devices, and safety gear.

Child Trailers

There are several child trailers on the market for towing smaller kids behind your bike. Most trailers can carry up to two children, but check the weight limits. Trailers sit low to the ground, making falls less likely, and you can also use them for carrying cargo and dogs. Trailers might have a higher resale value than other child-carrying devices. I have been on several fun trips with parents who towed their kids behind in a trailer. On one ride, my sister-in-law rented a bike with a trailer, put her 18-month-old and 4-year-old in the back, and off we went. No problem. Pack a few toys, some snacks, and juice boxes, and the kids have a blast. Often they fall asleep. But they don't like it when you pass by a playground.

Child Seats

Child seats mounted onto the back of the bike are another way to take smaller kids along. Child seats are less expensive than trailers, but they might require two adults to get going: one to hold the bike and one to load the kid. Make sure the seat is appropriate for your child's weight and size.

Tandem Bikes and Attached Tyke Bikes

Child-size cranks can be installed to adapt an adult's tandem bike for an adult/child team. Or you can turn your bike into a tandem by getting a tag-along children's bike. This one-wheeled trailer bike attaches to your bike's rear axle, giving your child an opportunity to do some pedaling.

For More Information

For maps, news, and other trip-planning tools, visit the National Park Service's Grand Canyon website at www.nps.gov/grca/ or call (928) 638-7888 for recorded visitor information.

A tandem with a child trailer is a good choice for family bike touring.

How To Use This Guide

This book is divided into two sections, "Part One: The South Rim" and "Part Two: The North Rim." Information on lodging, camping, dining, access, and other noteworthy topics appears at the beginning of each section, along with an overview map of the area.

Each ride is given a name and a number. Some of the names are official trail names; others are not, as I scouted and "found" the rides myself. I christened these rides as I saw fit. Each ride description includes route information, a difficulty rating, an elevation profile, and a map, which is sometimes combined with the map of other nearby rides. In order to keep this book lightweight and packable, descriptions of scenery and natural and human history have been kept to a minimum. Appendix D lists reading sources for more detailed information on the history and natural features of the area. Each ride is organized as follows:

This symbol marks the rides most appropriate for families. Equipment recommendations and other information in this section will help parents to determine which rides are good choices for their child's skill level. Use this information as a relative guideline only. You must make your own evaluation of your child's abilities. When in doubt, start with short rides or just turn around and head back as soon as a longer ride seems above your family's skill level.

Distance

The distance of each ride, measured in miles, is one-way unless the ride is a loop (in which case the round-trip mileage is given). Most of the distances listed here were taken from bicycle odometer readings. My odometer readings were sometimes slightly different from the mileage given on trail signs. Because of calibration differences, expect a margin of error between my cyclometer and yours. The track you take and changes in the trail because of trail maintenance and weather events might cause your odometer readings to differ from the mileages given in the book. With all of these factors in mind, you should plan for roughly a 0.2-mile margin of error.

Difficulty

Ratings used to show the difficulty of each ride are **Easy, Moderate,** and **Strenuous.** Difficulty is inherently relative to experience, physical conditioning, weather, attitude, and equipment. Difficulty ratings indicate the level of exertion required for each ride in terms of the uphill grade and the estimated mileage per hour. In determining difficulty ratings for this book, I have been very conservative. For example, a ride with a rating of Moderate will probably seem like an Easy ride for experienced mountain bikers.

Technical Rating

This rating system indicates the amount of technical mountain biking skill that is required on the ride. The ratings are **Beginner, Intermediate,** and **Advanced.** Again, in this book I have been very conservative in the rating. A ride rated as Intermediate will probably be considered a Beginner ride for experienced technical mountain bikers. The Beginner rating indicates that the surface is on pavement or very smooth track with few obstacles and few climbs or descents. The Intermediate rating indicates that the surface is rockier and could involve some steep or longer climbs during which beginners might need to dismount and walk their bikes a short distance. The Advanced rating is used to describe extremely rocky sections where most riders will have to dismount or "dab" their feet onto the ground to maintain balance. For the purposes of this book, if you have never ridden a bicycle off-pavement before, consider yourself a Beginner. If you enjoy single-track riding on rocky trails, your skills are at the Advanced level.

Type

This section describes the type of surface on which you will be biking. **Pavement** is a paved surface, either a trail or a road. **Double-track** refers to dirt or gravel roads, old or new. **Single-track** means you will be negotiating a narrow trail. The **Trail** and **Road** designations indicate whether or not motorized vehicles

The Kaibab National Forest—where ponderosa pine, rabbitbrush, and sage grow in abundance— is a prime location for mountain biking

share the route. The Road designation means that you should expect to have to share the route with automobiles. For example, Double-track/ Trail is an old dirt road that is closed to motorized vehicles, whereas Double-track/Road is a dirt road where you might find motorized vehicle traffic.

Season

This section lists the best times of the year to do the ride. Many routes on the South Rim are ridable all year except during extreme weather conditions. The North Rim is closed for most of the winter because of snow.

Maps

On the South Rim, the park's paved bike paths are kept clear of snow.

This section, which is included only for rides in more remote areas, lists maps that you might find helpful to use along with this guidebook.

Signage

Ratings of **Good**, **Fair**, or **Poor** accompany a description of what level of signing to expect on the trail. On rides rated as Poor, the signage is inconsistent and often nonexistent, so I suggest you carry the suggested supplemental maps on these rides.

Permits and Fees

Information on required permits, entrance fees, and reservations is provided if applicable.

Water Sources

Year-round, reliable water sources are listed where cyclists may consider car-camping or bikepacking. Assume that water treatment is required for all natural water sources.

Access to Trailhead

Directions for road access to trailheads are given from the nearest town or major paved road. The rides are designed so that you can reach the trailheads by normal passenger vehicle. However, high-clearance vehicles are usually better for traveling on Forest Service roads, especially during bad weather.

Trail Overview and Elevation Profiles

Trail Overviews give a general description of the surface, scenery, highlights, and hazards found on the rides. Elevation profiles indicate the amount of overall elevation gain and loss on each ride. They are best used as guides to help you decide which direction of travel is most desirable. The profile line represents the average change in elevation between regularly spaced intervals, *not the actual contours of the trail.* Don't let what looks like a flat section in a profile fool you. Some of the routes contain short climbs and steep descents that do not show up on the profile, and a series of steep climbs can be more tiring than one long, grinding ascent. For example, the short or gradual climbs mentioned at miles 1.6, 2.7, and 5.7 in the Route Description for Ride 15 do not appear on the profile below. Always consult the Route Description for detailed information about the topography of the trail. Information for the elevation profiles was obtained from USGS 7.5-minute quadrangles.

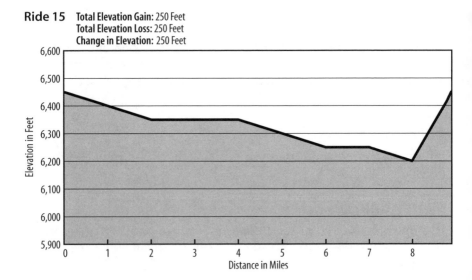

Ride 15 **Total Elevation Gain:** 250 Feet
Total Elevation Loss: 250 Feet
Change in Elevation: 250 Feet

Ride Maps

Maps of some rides are combined with those of other nearby rides. Check the map page reference at the beginning of each ride to easily locate the appropriate map. The following symbols are used on ride maps:

– – -	Featured Trail	△	Mountain
- - -	Hiking Trail	▮	Building
——	Railroad Tracks	⅌	Picnic Area
◯	Trailhead	⅄	Campground
4	Ride Number	◉	Bus Stop
	Grand Canyon National Park	Ⓟ	Parking Area
	Grand Canyon Inner Canyon	♨	Water Source
	National Forest	◯	Town
	Wilderness Area	⑥⓪	US Highway
	Indian Reservation	⑥⓪	State Highway

Route Description

The route for each ride is described in detail, with mileages listed for both directions of travel. Mileages might differ slightly from those of official sources, such as signs on the trail, because of the variances between a bicycle odometer reading and other methods of estimating distance. You should plan for at least a 0.2-mile margin of error because of minor route variations and calibration differences.

Directions given such as "west" or "northeast" are not absolute compass bearings, but approximate directional guides. Cattle guards and powerlines are sometimes mentioned in the Route Descriptions because they are permanent landmarks that are important for route finding. Route directions, scenic highlights, side trips, interesting local facts, and potential campsites and water sources are also given.

Rides for the Long-Distance Biker

A long-distance traveler by heart, I couldn't resist listing a few routes that would make exciting long-distance routes for those interested in bikepacking. I have described these routes briefly in Appendix A.

Part One: The South Rim

SOUTH RIM OVERVIEW

Getting There

You can get to the South Rim by plane, train, bus, bike, or automobile—take your pick. If you're arriving by car or bike, take I-40 to Williams (Exit 165) and head north on AZ 64. If you're coming from Flagstaff, take US 180 northwest to its junction with AZ 64 and turn right (north).

For most of its length, the Greenway Trail follows the edge of the South Rim.

Greyhound Bus Lines offers nationwide service to and from Flagstaff and Williams, Arizona; Grand Canyon Coaches offers service between those towns and the Grand Canyon. Call (928) 638-0821 for prices and more information. Transcanyon Shuttle makes a daily trip between the North and South Rims. Make your reservation by calling (928) 638-2820. Taxi service is available to and from trailheads, as well as the Grand Canyon National Park Airport in Tusayan. Call (928) 638-2822 or (928) 638-2631.

Relatively inexpensive flights to the Grand Canyon National Park Airport depart from Las Vegas, Los Angeles, and Phoenix. Visit www.scenic.com or call Scenic Airlines at (800) 634-6801 for flight schedules, prices, and information on packing your bike.

Grand Canyon Railway offers service from Williams. Call (800) THE-TRAIN or visit www.thetrain.com for more information.

Staying There

Hotels

There are several hotels inside the park as well as in Tusayan, just outside the park. If you plan to visit during the busy summer season, be sure to book your room well in advance. For reservations inside the park, call (888) 297-2757 or visit www.nps.gov/grca/.

Camping

There are several developed (fee) campgrounds both in and near the park. Inside the park, camping is permitted only in designated areas. Mather Campground in Grand Canyon Village (South Rim Village) often fills up during the summer months; call (800) 365-2267 for reservations. The campground at Desert View is available on a first-come, first-served basis.

Camping choices outside the park are Camper Village in Tusayan, (928) 638-2887, and Ten-X Campground in the Kaibab National Forest, (928) 638-2443. Primitive car-camping in the national forest is allowed in designated areas. There are plenty of camping options near the Grandview Lookout Trailhead (see Ride 11, p. 72).

Day-Use Fees

The National Park Service charges $20 per vehicle for a seven-day pass. Pedestrians, bicyclists, motorcyclists, and members of organized groups pay $10 per person for a seven-day pass. The Grand Canyon Pass, which grants unlimited park access for a year, is $40. Currently, there is no day-use fee for national forest lands.

Food, Supplies, and Other Amenities

There are many stores and restaurants inside and outside the park. The General Store, a relatively large grocery store inside the park, sells most everything you will need including camping and hiking gear. You'll find showers and laundry facilities near Mather Campground. The National Park Service plans to offer bike rental services in the park sometime in the future, but, for the moment, the nearest bike shops are in Flagstaff, Arizona (see Appendix B).

Information

If you need more information while you are in the area, you can stop by one of these places:

• Tusayan Ranger District Office, Kaibab National Forest (USFS): East of AZ 64, north of Tusayan, and south of the park entrance, (928) 638-2443, www.fs.fed.us/r3/kai/ (see South Rim Overview map, p. 36).

• Canyon View Information Plaza (NPS): Currently accessible by foot, bike, or wheelchair-accessible shuttle bus only, www.nps.gov/grca (see Rides 4 and 5 map, p. 50).

• Backcountry Information Center (NPS): Maswik Transportation Center, (928) 638-7875, www.nps.gov/grca/backcountry/ (see Rides 4 and 5 map, p. 50).

Midnight at the El Tovar

When I was a park ranger at the Grand Canyon, I heard several locals talk about the creep-out factor at the El Tovar Hotel. Perched at the edge of the canyon, the hotel does possess an unsettling quality. I had always attributed this feeling to the imposing architecture in the style of old European hunting lodges, until another Grand Canyon–area resident told me that she knew someone who had seen a ghost at the El Tovar.

The name "El Tovar" comes from the Spaniard who, depending on which book you read, may or may not have been the first European to gaze into the daunting depths of the Grand Canyon. Built in 1905, the El Tovar once ranked among the most luxurious hotels in the West. In those days, that distinction meant it offered guests running water and indoor restrooms. A century later, things haven't changed that much: Anybody who is anybody stays at the El Tovar while on a trip to the Grand Canyon.

El Tovar Hotel entrance.

On the outside, the building resembles a stately Rhine castle. Tall posts with club-shaped tips barricade all the balconies. Because the hotel attracts more than its share of lightning strikes, each post is equipped with its own lightning rod. When you enter the perpetual darkness of the lobby, you'll see the interior design of a trophy hunter gone mad. From the walls, mounted animal heads glare down at the oblivious tourists mingling around the fireplace. I could see why the hotel creeps some people out, but I needed more proof before I could believe the hotel was haunted. So, I decided to go ghost hunting.

First, I spoke with Thomas Ratz, a night waiter at the El Tovar for more than 20 years, to see if he had any good stories to tell.

"Well, there's the man wearing a hat and long coat. He's very popular. Some say the man in the long coat is Fred Harvey [whose company helped build the El Tovar], but he died before the hotel was built—so that's a little silly, don't you think?"

"Maybe he just wants to see how the place turned out," I suggested. "Have you seen him?" I asked.

"Oh, no," Ratz laughed. "It sure looks like a haunted house, but I've never seen a ghost here. Maybe I'm just not sensitive to that kind of thing."

My chat with the concierge revealed more tales of unusual phenomena. One couple had checked out in a hurry after they saw skulls staring at them from the mirrors in their room. A cleaning crew had witnessed a big ball of light open the kitchen doors, move across the dining room, and then float out the glass windows and into the canyon. From others, I heard accounts of two poltergeist-like boys who knock over merchandise in the gift shop next door, an attic tower that no one wants to enter alone, an elevator that smells of blood, and a night watchman who became an eyewitness to a ghost.

A fan of cold, hard facts, I felt the need to personally interview the eyewitness to the ghost. A longtime resident of Grand Canyon Village, he spoke with me on condition of anonymity because he's afraid people will think he's a little flaky. But I assure you, this man was sober and of sound mind when he told me the following:

"A few winters ago, the hotel was closed for renovations. We were gutting out the rooms on one side of the corridor. So, on one side all the doors were missing. Working late at night, I'd be the last to leave for the day and was responsible for checking all the hallways before locking up. I'd glance into each room as I walked by to make sure it was clear. I'd gotten eerie feelings before, lots of creaking and sounds of people walking around even though I knew I was the only one in the building. There would be nights when I would have to leave before finishing my security check because it was just too creepy.

"One night, while I was walking down the north corridor on the third floor, I passed one of the suites and saw a woman standing there in a faint blue gown, 1930s style, staring right back at me. The woman didn't say anything. She just stared at me. Startled, I jumped back. When I looked again, she was gone."

What he saw that night scared him so badly that he ran straight home to his wife, his hands shaking, his face pale, and told her the same story he told me.

Go see for yourself. Breakfast at the El Tovar restaurant is the best in town, there is a cozy sitting room on the second floor perfect for sipping coffee on chilly mornings, and the bar has a porch with a canyon view. Before you leave, be sure to cross the street in front of the hotel and walk toward the fire hydrant near the center of the parking lot. Look for the gray slab of marble hidden in the shadows under a juniper tree. You might have to dust off the pine needles in order to read the words inscribed in the stone: "Pirl A. Ward 1879–1934." According to the staff, no one knows who she was or why she's buried there—or why a woman in 1930s-style dress roams the hallways during lonely winter nights at the El Tovar Hotel.

If the stories are true, an unregistered guest might be roaming the hallways of the El Tovar Hotel, which perches on the edge of the Grand Canyon.

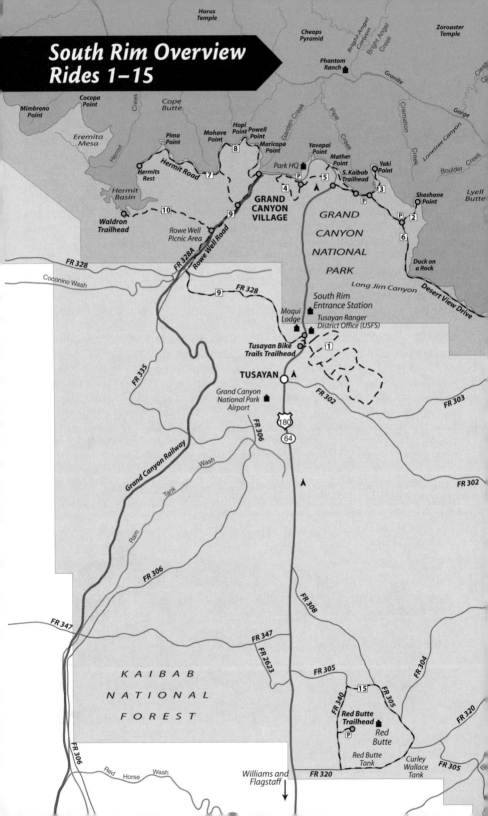

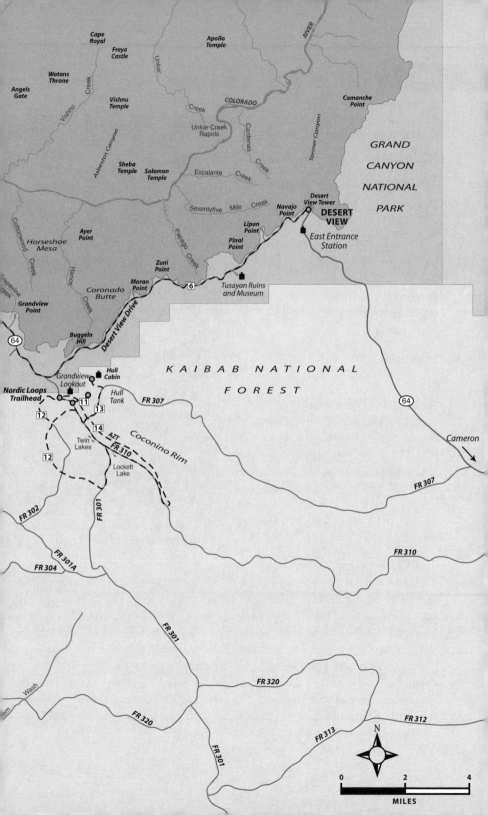

Ride 1 ▶ TUSAYAN LOOPS

See map, p. 40

Distance: 3.6 to 10.7 miles

Difficulty: Easy to Moderate

Technical Rating: Intermediate

Type: Single-track/Trail

Season
All year except when the trail is muddy or snow-covered.

Maps
USFS Recreation Map: Kaibab National Forest

Signage
Good.

Access to Trailhead
Trailhead parking for the Tusayan Bike Trails Trailhead is on the west side of AZ 64, just north of Tusayan and 1.2 miles south of Grand Canyon National Park's South Rim Entrance Station. Look for the trailhead sign, where maps and a trail register are available.

Trail maps and a register are available at the Tusayan Bike Trails Trailhead.

Trail Overview
This one is for the mountain bikers! The Forest Service has built some fine trails here for mountain bikers of all levels to enjoy. Highlights of these trails include wildflowers, pleasant single track, and frequent elk sightings. (Note that although these trails are not very technical, I have rated them as intermediate compared with the other rides on the South Rim.)

Just south of the trailhead is the gateway town of Tusayan (Too-say-on), named after the Tusayan Indian ruins near Desert View. If you want a longer ride, at mile 5.7 on Loop 3, you can continue farther on a mostly single-track trail through ponderosa forests to the trailhead at Grandview Lookout—a total of 16.4 miles one way from the Tusayan Bike Trails Trailhead.

Route Description

Mile

0.0/10.7   From the trailhead parking area, get on the single track that heads north from the sign. Take note of the brown Carsonite posts that are marked Trail #1, #2, and #3, each with a bicycle sticker. Use these signs to navigate this trail system.

0.1/10.6   Make a short, steep descent. Beginners might want to walk their bikes here.

0.2/10.5   Go right (east) and under the highway through the concrete culvert. Watch for glass. After going through the tunnel, close the gate behind you.

0.7/10.0   The trail heads mostly due east. Note several access paths from Tusayan joining the trail.

0.8/9.9   The end of Loop 1 meets the trail here. Stay right (east).

1.0/9.7   The beginning of Loop 1 heads left (northeast). For Loops 2 and 3, go right onto the double track.

Loop   *Loop 1: If you are doing Loop 1, an excellent 3.6-mile loop, go left (northeast) at mile 1.0 and head up the hard-packed gravel road. At mile 1.6 (0.6 miles from mile 1.0), turn left, then make an immediate left (follow the signs) onto the single-track trail. After a brief climb, the trail winds through a shady forest of pines—a truly enjoyable section of the route. At 2.6 miles, you meet back up with the trail that leads to Loops 2 and 3. Here you can go right (back the way you came) to return to the Tusayan Bike Trails Trailhead, or go left onto the double track to continue on the longer Loops 2 and 3.*

Loop   *Loops 2 and 3: For Loops 2 and 3, go right at mile 1.0 onto the double track. After a steep climb, the old double-track road assumes a gradual grade as it heads south.*

1.7/9.0   The town of Tusayan is visible to the right (southwest). Stay left. The trail soon begins to head east as it enters a shallow limestone canyon where you might see examples of the many fossils that are found in the Kaibab Formation.

2.3/8.4   This is where you will rejoin the trail at the end of Loops 2 and 3.

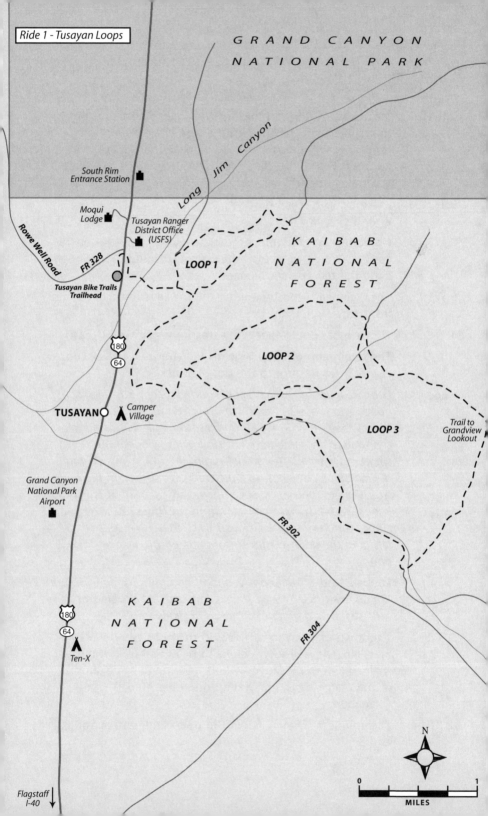

Ride 1   Total Elevation Gain: 250 Feet
Total Elevation Loss: 250 Feet
Change in Elevation: 200 Feet

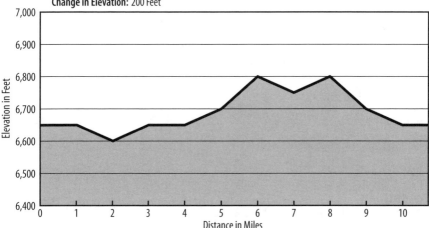

Mile

3.8/6.9   If you want a slightly shorter loop, take Loop 2 here by going up and left (northeast). For Loop 3, continue straight ahead. You soon travel through a field of rabbit-brush and sage. Pass by two stock tanks.

4.6/6.1   As you continue on Loop 3, look for a signpost directing you to the left (north) side of a treatment plant. Keep along the line of trees until you see another sign, which directs you left (north) into a narrow drainage. Then make a steady, but very doable, climb up the drainage.

5.7/5.0   To stay on Loop 3, turn left where the trail intersects FR 2709. Loop 3 follows this road on its way west. (You will see a sign for the trail that leads to Grandview Lookout; see Trail Overview.)

6.0/4.7   Loop 2 joins the trail here.

6.9/3.8   As the road begins to climb, look for a sign directing you off FR 2709 and onto a dirt track to the left. The dirt track climbs a short, steep, rocky hill. After the initial climbing, you cruise through a forest along a quiet old road that meanders on a mostly downhill grade.

8.4/2.3   You are back at the section of trail described at mile 2.3. Go right and ride back the way you came.

9.7/1.0   Loop 1 rejoins the trail here.

10.7/0.0   Your ride ends at the parking lot at the Tusayan Bike Trails Trailhead.

Ride 2 *SHOSHONE POINT*

See map, p. 44.

 **This trail makes a great introduction to double-track riding.**

Distance: 1.2 miles

Difficulty: Easy

Technical Rating: Beginner

Type: Double-track/Trail

Season
All year except when the trail is covered in snow.

Signage
Good.

Permits and Fees
$10–$20 for a seven-day park pass; $40 for a pass good for a year. Park visitors can obtain a permit to reserve Shoshone Point for special events.

Access to Trailhead
From Desert View Intersection (Desert View Drive and South Entrance Road) in the park, go east on Desert View Drive (AZ 64), following the signs for Yaki Point and Desert View. The parking area for Shoshone Point

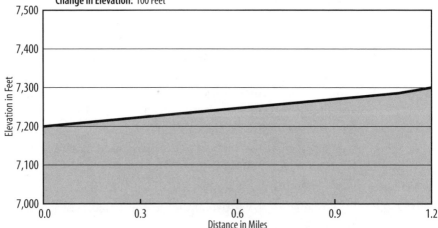

Ride 2   Total Elevation Gain: 100 Feet
Total Elevation Loss: 0 Feet
Change in Elevation: 100 Feet

is 2.1 miles farther on the north side of the road, just past the second picnic area and east of mile marker 244. The trail description starts at the parking area.

Trail Overview

Children 10 and older should be able to handle this short ride to Shoshone Point, possibly named for the Shoshonean language spoken by the Southern Paiute Indians. At the end of this easy ride, walk the short path to end of the narrow peninsula of Shoshone Point. Locals treasure the panoramic view from what is perhaps the best overlook on the South Rim.

Park visitors can obtain a permit to reserve Shoshone Point for special events such as weddings. The NPS allows hikers and bikers to use this road when permit holders have not reserved the area. If you see cars filling the parking lot, however, you should give the permit holders some privacy and come back another time.

Route Description

Mile

0.0/1.2 Go around the gate and head northeast on the dirt road.

0.1/1.1 The grade gradually ascends uphill all the way to the end. I've seen fantastic blooms of lupine here in the summer.

1.2/0.0 The trail bends to the north just before you reach the picnic area. Technically, the tables and restrooms here are for the use of permit holders only.

A short hiking trail leads to Shoshone Point and one of the South Rim's best views.

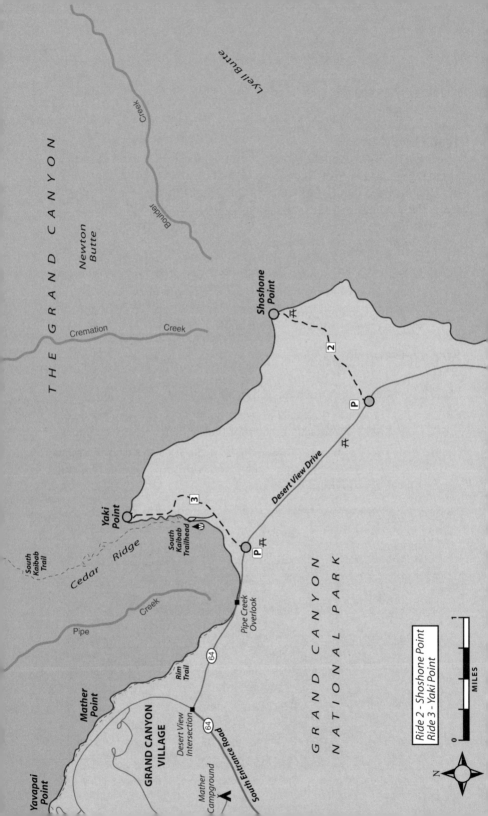

THE GRAND CANYON

Lyell Butte

Creek

Boulder

Newton Butte

Cremation   Creek

Shoshone Point

2

Desert View Drive

Yaki Point

South Kaibab Trail

Cedar Ridge

South Kaibab Trailhead

3

W

P

Pipe   Creek

Pipe Creek Overlook

64

Rim Trail

Mather Point

Yavapai Point

GRAND CANYON VILLAGE

Desert View Intersection

64

South Entrance Road

Mather Campground

GRAND CANYON NATIONAL PARK

Ride 2 - Shoshone Point
Ride 3 - Yaki Point

MILES

0   1

N

Ride 3 **YAKI POINT**

Excellent ride for children who can handle the short distance, as well as for adults pulling kids in trailers.

Distance: 1.2 miles

Difficulty: Easy

Technical Rating: Beginner

Type: Pavement/Road

Season All year.

Signage Good.

Permits and Fees $10–$20 for a seven-day park pass; $40 for a pass good for a year.

Interpretive signs at Yaki Point highlight geologic features and facts about natural and cultural history.

Access to Trailhead

From Desert View Intersection (Desert View Drive and South Entrance Road) in the park, go east on Desert View Drive (AZ 64), following the signs for Yaki Point and Desert View. In 1.2 miles, you will find a parking lot and picnic area on the right (south) side of the road. The trail description starts at this picnic area, which is just east of the turnoff for Yaki Point.

Trail Overview

With the exception of the occasional shuttle bus, the road out to Yaki Point is closed to vehicle traffic during the summer—making it a great family ride to a quiet overlook. Those looking for a longer ride can extend it by adding the route described in Ride 5: Greenway Trail to Pipe Creek Overlook (see p. 51). Or you can bring the bike locks, ride to the South Kaibab Trailhead, and take the short, strenuous hike to the breathtaking view at Ooh Aah Point (0.75 mile one way).

When you look out from Yaki Point, you are looking down at Cremation Canyon, named for the cremated remains of prehistoric

Indians found in this side canyon. From the overlook at Yaki Point, the North Rim is about 10 miles away by air but a rugged 24-mile hike by land. Mule packers use the South Kaibab Trail below to get supplies to and from Phantom Ranch. From the overlook, you can see sections of the South Kaibab, one of the steepest trails in the Grand Canyon.

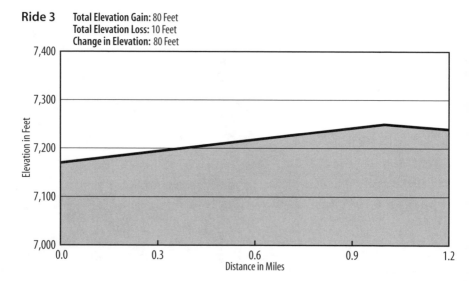

Ride 3   Total Elevation Gain: 80 Feet
Total Elevation Loss: 10 Feet
Change in Elevation: 80 Feet

Route Description

Mile

0.0/1.2   From the picnic area just east of the road to Yaki Point, bike west along Desert View Drive (AZ 64).

0.1/1.1   Turn right (north) on the road to Yaki Point. This road should be quiet during the summer, but stay alert for tour buses and park vehicles.

0.5/0.7   The road to the left leads a short distance to the South Kaibab Trailhead and Ooh Aah Point.

1.2/0.0   Yaki Point Overlook offers views of the South Kaibab Trail to your left and Cremation Canyon to your right. Interpretive signs point out other canyon features. Turn around and go back the way you came.

Ride 4 **_RANGER LOOP_**

See map, p. 50.

This is an excellent path for family rides.

Distance: 3.2 miles

Difficulty: Easy

Technical Rating: Beginner

Type: Pavement/Trail

Season
All year except when the path is snow-covered.

Signage
None at the time of printing, but the path is easy to follow.

Permits and Fees
$10–$20 for a seven-day park pass; $40 for a pass good for a year.

Access to Trailhead
The trail description starts at the Market Plaza/Yavapai Lodge parking area in the center of Grand Canyon Village (South Rim Village).

The paved paths of the South Rim offer the ultimate kid-friendly biking experience.

Ride 4   **Total Elevation Gain:** 50 Feet
             Total Elevation Loss: 50 Feet
             Change in Elevation: 50 Feet

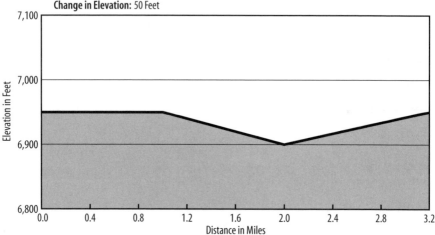

Trail Overview

I call this bike path Ranger Loop because park rangers and other park employees routinely jog or bike this route as part of their physical fitness training. The paved path makes a nice family ride through peaceful piñon-juniper forest. You'll get glimpses of housing areas for 1,500 or so people: some of the park employees and their families. Please respect their privacy and stay on the loop outside this residential area.

Route Description

Mile

0.0/3.2   From the Market Plaza/Yavapai Lodge parking area, look for a paved bike path that descends from the parking lot on the south side of the grocery store. The path is across from the deli.

0.1/3.1   Stay right. Two access trails to the left lead to a campground.

0.2/3.0   The path intersects with Zuni Road here. To do the loop, go straight (west); the path to the left leads to the campground, and the one to the right leads to Park Headquarters. After crossing Zuni Road, head left and up. When you see paths leading into the residential area, stay on the outside loop.

0.9/2.3   The path crosses Bob Mann and Randy Thompson Streets before crossing Clinic Road. Continue to follow the outside loop as it begins to go north.

1.5/1.7   Cross Park Circle.

Mile

1.7/1.5	On your right, look for the NPS mule barn, home of the pack mules that haul supplies to the rangers at the Phantom Ranch and Indian Garden Ranger Stations.
1.9/1.3	The ranger patrol horses live here.
2.0/1.2	Cross Tonto/Juniper Street, then follow the path down. Stay to the right (east) of the large, brown Ranger Operations building.
2.1/1.1	At the intersection with Village Loop Road, go right (east) to stay on the path.
2.2/1.0	The path crosses Navajo Street and then goes in front of the library. Glide through a shady grove of ponderosa pines.
3.0/0.2	Park Headquarters, the park graveyard, and a short hiking path to the rim are on your left (north). Cross the road and continue straight ahead.
3.2/0.0	A short path to the right takes you up to the post office and back to where you started.

Native Americans of the Grand Canyon

Six modern tribes—the Hopi, Navajo, Zuni, Southern Paiute, Hualapai, and Havasupai—link their histories with the Grand Canyon. Hopi ancestry extends back to the Anasazi, the ancient people who began to build homes in the canyon around A.D. 800. The Navajo, the largest Native American tribe in the United States, trace their roots to sometime after A.D. 1000. The Zuni still consider certain sites in the Grand Canyon as sacred to their culture, even though the Zuni Indian Reservation lies many miles to the east (south of Gallup, New Mexico). The North Rim is part of the historic lands of the Southern Paiute. The Hualapai tribe owns nearly one million acres of land on the Coconino Plateau and west of the park.

But despite ancestral connections to so many tribes, today the Grand Canyon remains home to only one: the Havasupai. Known as the "people of the blue-green water," the Havasupai live at the bottom of the canyon on a reservation surrounded by parklands. Their home, which includes the surreal turquoise waters of Havasu Creek, is possibly the most beautiful place on earth.

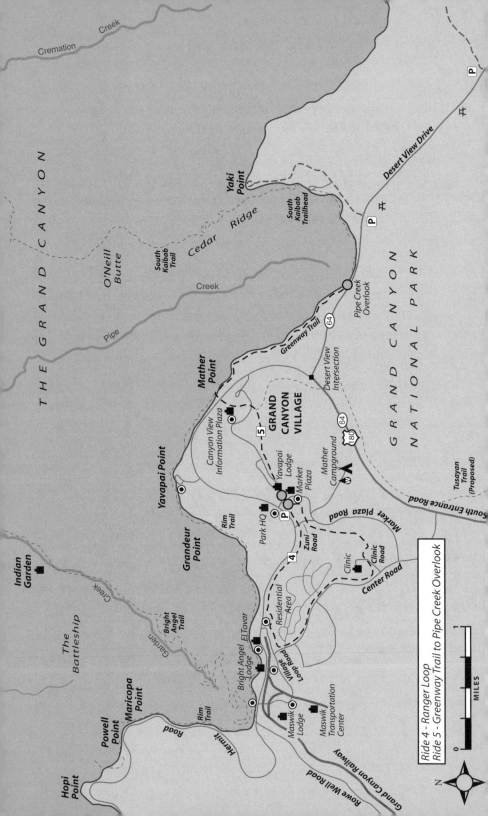

Ride 4 - Ranger Loop
Ride 5 - Greenway Trail to Pipe Creek Overlook

Ride 5 GREENWAY TRAIL TO PIPE CREEK OVERLOOK

The Greenway Trail: so many views, so little time.

 This is the perfect Grand Canyon family ride.

Distance: 2.5 miles

Difficulty: Easy

Technical Rating: Beginner

Type: Pavement/Trail

Season
All year.

Signage
Good.

Permits and Fees
$10–$20 for a seven-day park pass; $40 for a pass good for a year.

Access to Trailhead
The route description begins at the Market Plaza/Yavapai Lodge parking area in the center of Grand Canyon Village (South Rim Village).

Trail Overview

A couple on a tandem bike hauling their 2-year-old in a trailer joined me on this ride, so I can attest to the family-friendly aspect of this bike path. The path involves some climbing but it's short enough to keep it easy. The unbeatable views along the rim should charm adrenaline-seeking mountain bikers, as well.

This trip includes a stop at the Canyon View Information Plaza, where you can catch a shuttle bus, ask a ranger questions, or shop at the bookstore. In the future, bike rentals should also be available here. You can see a small section of the Colorado River from nearby Mather Point, which is named after Stephen T. Mather, the first director of the National Park Service.

At the end of the ride is Pipe Creek Overlook—hopefully the future start of a greenway that will lead all the way to Desert View. Pipe Creek's odd name resulted from a practical joke. In 1894, pioneering entrepreneur Ralph Cameron found a pipe in the creek near the bottom of the canyon. He scratched a false date on the pipe and placed it where the hikers behind him would find it. When his friends found the pipe, they were excited by the 100-year-old "artifact" they had found, until Cameron let them in on the joke.

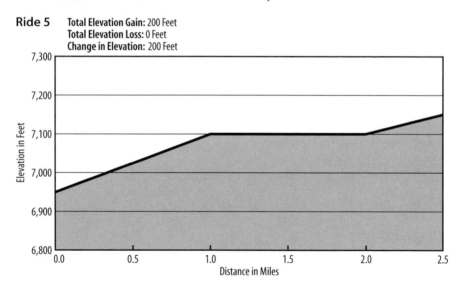

Ride 5   Total Elevation Gain: 200 Feet
Total Elevation Loss: 0 Feet
Change in Elevation: 200 Feet

Route Description

Mile

0.0/2.5   From the parking area, go to the bike path in front (north) of the Yavapai Lodge lobby. Head right (northeast) onto the bike path.

0.8/1.7   The path climbs before it crosses the road to Canyon View Information Plaza. You soon enter the plaza, where you'll find a visitor center, a bus stop, a bookstore, and restrooms.

1.1/1.4   Cross the road at the crosswalk to access Mather Point, the beginning of the Greenway Trail, which heads east. All the overlooks here are worth walking out to before you continue your bike ride. Note that the Rim Trail between Mather Point and Hermits Rest to the west is closed to bicycles. As of this printing, the National Park Service is planning trails that will be open to bicycling—but in the meantime, watch for signs marking park trails that are closed to bicycle traffic.

1.5/1.0   Stop at the bend in the path to check out the hard-to-beat view of the canyon. Look for Bright Angel Canyon and Zoroaster Temple to the north. At the bottom of the canyon, the green tops of the cottonwood trees at Phantom Ranch are visible. Yaki Point is the ridgeline to the east. Look for the trail that skirts the side of the canyon. This is the South Kaibab Trail, which hardy hikers use to reach Phantom Ranch. After you leave the bend in the path, more views open up as you travel over some roller-coaster hills.

2.5/0.0   At the time of this printing, the Greenway Trail ends here at Pipe Creek Overlook, also called Pipe Creek Vista or First Pullout.

Ride 6 ▶ *DESERT VIEW DRIVE*
See map, p. 57.

Distance: 24.3 miles

Difficulty: Moderate

Technical Rating: Beginner

Type: Pavement/Road

Season
All year.

Signage
Good.

Permits and Fees
$10–$20 for a seven-day park pass;
$40 for a pass good for a year.

Access to Trailhead
The trail description starts at the
Market Plaza/Yavapai Lodge parking
area in the center of Grand Canyon
Village (South Rim Village). The end
of the trail is at the Desert View
Tower complex parking area on
AZ 64, just beyond the park's
East Entrance Station.

Bikers can get information on park bike paths at the Canyon Village Information Plaza.

Trail Overview
Until the National Park Service completes the proposed greenway along
the East Rim beyond Pipe Creek Overlook, those interested in the
24-mile ride out to Desert View from Grand Canyon Village will have
to travel Desert View Drive (AZ 64), alternately East Rim Drive. This
road ride is long but not difficult for most cyclists, although they must
endure the traffic and narrow shoulders.

This route offers several opportunities for short side trips to canyon
overlooks, and a historic watchtower designed by architect Mary Colter
anchors the end. Colter loosely based Desert View Tower's design on
Indian ruins she had seen in the Four Corners region. Built in 1922, the
tower was designed to function as a gift shop and tourist site, and it
continues to serve those purposes today. Walk up the stairs to check out
the view from the top.

Route Description

Mile

0.0/24.3 From the parking area, go to the bike path in front (north) of the Yavapai Lodge lobby. Head right (northeast) onto the bike path.

0.8/23.5 The path climbs before it crosses the road to Canyon View Information Plaza. You soon enter the plaza, where you'll find a visitor center, a bus stop, a bookstore, and restrooms.

1.1/23.2 Cross the road at the crosswalk to access Mather Point, the beginning of the Greenway Trail, which heads east. All the overlooks here are worth walking out to before you continue your bike ride. Note that the Rim Trail between Mather Point and Hermits Rest to the west is closed to bicycles. As of this printing, the National Park Service is planning trails that will be open to bicycling—but in the meantime, watch for signs marking park trails that are closed to bicycle traffic.

1.5/22.8 Stop at the bend in the path to check out the hard-to-beat view of the canyon. Look for Bright Angel Canyon and Zoroaster Temple to the north. At the bottom of the canyon, the green tops of the cottonwood trees at Phantom Ranch are visible. Yaki Point is the ridgeline to the east. Look for the trail that skirts the side of the canyon. This is the South Kaibab Trail, which hardy hikers use to reach Phantom Ranch. After you leave the bend in the path, more views open up as you travel over some roller-coaster hills.

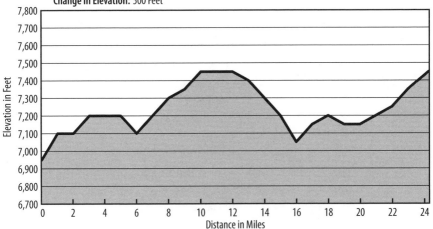

Ride 6   **Total Elevation Gain:** 1,050 Feet
Total Elevation Loss: 550 Feet
Change in Elevation: 500 Feet

The Desert View Tower at the end of this ride is a classic Grand Canyon tourist stop.

Mile

2.5/21.8   At the time of this printing, the Greenway Trail on which you have been traveling ends here at Pipe Creek Overlook, also called Pipe Creek Vista or First Pullout. So, for now you must continue on Desert View Drive.

3.0/21.3   Here you pass the road to Yaki Point (see Ride 3, p. 45).

4.4/19.9   The dirt road here is a short ride out to Shoshone Point (see Ride 2, p. 42).

6.0/18.3   Rangers call the pullout here Duck on a Rock, named after a rock formation that once resembled a duck—until a piece of it fell off.

8.2/16.1   Pass a picnic area on the north side of the road.

10.8/13.5   Here is the spur road to Grandview Point.

11.5/12.8   In this area, look for dirt pullouts that mark the former site of the Grandview Hotel. Faint paths into the forest on the north side of the road lead to the historic foundations of the hotel, which closed after the developments at Grand Canyon Village drew customers away.

12.9/11.4   This road (FR 310) leads to the Arizona Trail and the bike trails that start at the Grandview Lookout Trailhead (see Ride 11: Vishnu Overlook Loop, p. 72).

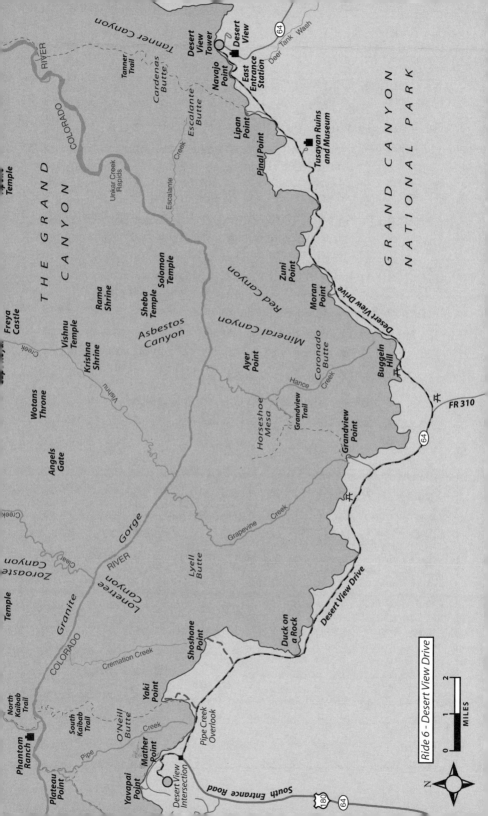

Ride 6 – Desert View Drive

MILES
0   1   2

N

Mile

14.0/10.3	Start the 1.0-mile descent down Buggeln Hill. Admire the views of the San Francisco Peaks to the southeast.
14.3/10.0	Pass the Buggeln Picnic Area.
17.0/7.3	This is the road to Moran Point, which bears the name of Thomas Moran, the late-19th- and early-20th-century artist best known for his paintings of the Grand Canyon and other natural wonders in the American West.
20.9/3.4	A short road to the right (south) leads to the Tusayan Ruins. Take the self-guided path to the ruins and museum, which are well worth the stop.
22.2/2.1	From Lipan Point, the trailhead for the Tanner Trail, you can see the Unkar Creek Rapids in the Colorado River.
23.4/0.9	Here you reach Navajo Point.
24.3/0.0	You can see the stone tower just before you reach the road to the facilities at Desert View. Take this road left (north). Unless you have arranged for a personal shuttle, be sure to stop at the snack bar for some ice cream before you start the long haul back to Grand Canyon Village.

Tusayan Ruins

Built around A.D. 1185, the pueblo at the Tusayan Ruins site sits 0.25 mile from the canyon rim. Archaeologists believe that a community of about 30 people lived here for 20 years before migrating south and east. "Anasazi" is the Navajo word for the ancient people who inhabited these and the other 2,000 or so Grand Canyon–area ruins. From the museum, take the short paved path that leads to the ruins. Rangers lead guided hikes to the Tusayan Ruins several times a day during the summer months.

The museum at the Tusayan Ruins site is worth a stop.

Ride 7 **HERMIT ROAD**

See map, p. 66.

See map, p. 66.

This route is especially good for riders on tandems or pulling trailers.

Distance: 8.2 miles

Difficulty: Easy

Technical Rating: Beginner

Type: Pavement/Road

Season
All year.

Signage
Good on Hermit Road. Poor on dirt roads.

Permits and Fees
$10–$20 for a seven-day park pass; $40 for a pass good for a year.

Access to Trailhead
The route description starts at the intersection of Hermit Road (West Rim Drive) and the Village Loop at the Village Route Transfer bus stop. Nearby parking is available at Maswik Transportation Center, Bright Angel Lodge, and in the gravel lot on the south side of the train tracks.

The steps of the Powell Memorial lead to views of Horn Creek and the Orphan Mine.

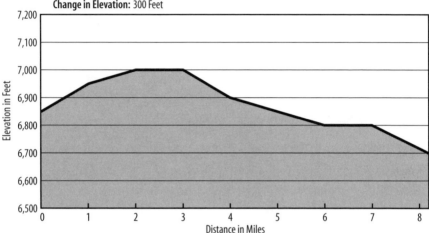

Ride 7   Total Elevation Gain: 150 Feet
Total Elevation Loss: 300 Feet
Change in Elevation: 300 Feet

Trail Overview

Hermit Road, a.k.a. West Rim Drive, is fun to bike, especially during the summer when the road is closed to all vehicles except tour buses and those with handicapped placards. I've seen elk, condors, and deer while riding this road, all in one day!

The hiking trail along the rim is closed to bicycles, so be sure to stay on the road, which skirts the canyon for most of the route. Park regulations require bicyclists on Hermit Road to pull over for passing buses. To avoid having to pull over too often, try starting your ride just after a tour bus leaves the Village Route Transfer Stop. The good news is that most shuttle buses have bike racks mounted on the front—so you can catch a ride if you get tired. Keep in mind that the buses stop at all stops when going west, but when going east they only stop at Hermits Rest, Hopi Point, and the Village Route Transfer Stop.

At the end of the ride, Hermits Rest is a charming place to refresh. In 1914, architect Mary Colter designed the building using natural materials from the area. She intended it to look like a hermit's cave. The facility houses a gift shop and a snack bar, and winter travelers will really appreciate the chance to sip hot cocoa by the stone fireplace.

Route Description

Mile

0.0/8.2   From the Village Route Transfer Stop, go west on Hermit Road. Stay on the road, as the trail along the rim is for hikers only.

0.1/8.1   Rowe Well Road comes in from the left (southeast). Continue straight and make a significant climb onto the West Rim.

1.1/7.1   Trailview Overlook is the first bus stop you reach. Take the short walk to the overlook for an excellent view of the Bright Angel Trail, Grand Canyon Village, and the San Francisco Peaks in the distance.

1.7/6.5   At Maricopa Point, can you find the formation that is called The Battleship?

2.2/6.0   The concrete structure near the rim, the Powell Memorial, honors John Wesley Powell, the one-armed Civil War veteran who led the first government expedition down the wild rapids of the Colorado River in 1869. Climb the steps of the memorial for views of Horn Creek and the Orphan Mine, which was first worked for copper. Uranium was discovered there in 1954, and the mine remained open until 1966. Today the National Park Service owns it.

A rock arch welcomes travelers to Hermits Rest.

Mile

2.4/5.8	Hopi Point, a favorite place to watch the sunset, is one of the few stops where eastbound buses will pick you up. A long section of the Colorado River, including a portion of Granite Rapids, is visible to the west.
3.2/5.0	Here you reach Mohave Point.
4.2/4.0	The Abyss gives you a dizzying look over the steep canyon walls. On the east side of The Abyss, the Great Mohave Wall drops 3,000 feet to the Tonto Plateau below.
7.1/1.1	Pima Point—so many great views, so little time.
8.2/0.0	Be sure to stop in at Hermits Rest, home to my favorite gift shop in the entire park. From the bus stop, you can catch the bus back to where you started, or if you haven't had enough fun yet, turn around and ride back the way you came.

The California Condor

While biking Hermit Road, you might see California condors circling the sky above you. Sightings are common here, but not too long ago, the condor seemed destined for extinction. In 1987, the last three condors living in the wild were captured and placed into a captive breeding program at the San Diego Zoo. *After the successful reintroduction of condors in California, zoologists selected the Vermilion Cliffs (north of the North Rim) as another release site. Fossil evidence found in caves indicated to scientists that the Grand Canyon was historically a nesting area for these scavengers. Today more condors live at the Grand Canyon than existed in the entire world in 1982. About 22 of these birds, the largest in North America, now make the Grand Canyon their home.*

With wingspans of up to 10 feet, condors can travel as far as 100 miles in a day. Unlike vultures, condors use vision instead of smell to find the carcasses on which they feed. These gregarious birds travel together in flocks and are extremely curious about human activity. If you are curious about condor activity and are visiting during the summer, check the park newspaper for a schedule of informative, ranger-led talks. Photo by Ron Shaffer.

Ride 8 ABYSS LOOP

See map, p. 66.

Distance: 7.0 miles

Difficulty: Easy

Technical Rating: Beginner

Type: Pavement and Double-track/Road

Season
All year except when covered by snow.

Signage
Good on Hermit Road. Poor on dirt roads.

Permits and Fees
$10–$20 for a seven-day park pass; $40 for a pass good for a year.

Access to Trailhead
The route description starts at the intersection of Hermit Road (West Rim Drive) and the Village Loop at the Village Route Transfer bus stop. Nearby parking is

Ponderosa pines shade the way for a good portion of this loop.

available at Maswik Transportation Center, Bright Angel Lodge, and in the gravel lot on the south side of the train tracks.

Trail Overview
This loop takes you to one of my favorite Grand Canyon overlooks before it heads into the forest for some nice dirt-road riding. The Abyss lives up to its name. Unlike many of the other overlooks, The Abyss is at the head of a side canyon, rather than at the end of a peninsula. This unusual positioning gives you an impressive view of a dramatic drop-off into the canyon. Occasionally, ranger rescue helicopter pilots use this point to access the canyon in case of emergencies. The first time I was flown in this way, to a rescue emergency, I grabbed the seat in response to what seemed like the bottom of the world dropping out from under me.

Older kids who can ride geared bicycles might be able to do this ride. Hermit Road is fun to bike because, during the summer, it is closed to all vehicles except tour buses and those with handicapped placards. However, park regulations require bicyclists on Hermit Road to pull over for passing buses. To avoid having to pull over too often, try starting your ride just after a tour bus leaves the Village Route Transfer Stop. Keep in mind that the buses traveling the portion of Hermit Road included in this ride stop at all stops when going west, but when going east they only stop at Hopi Point and the Village Route Transfer Stop.

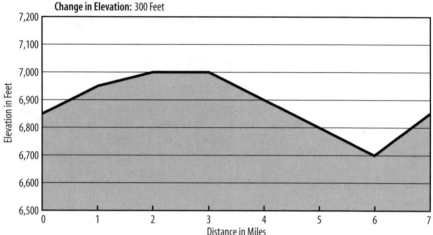

Ride 8   Total Elevation Gain: 300 Feet
Total Elevation Loss: 300 Feet
Change in Elevation: 300 Feet

Route Description

Mile

0.0/7.0   From the Village Route Transfer Stop, go west on Hermit Road. Stay on the road, as the trail along the rim is for hikers only.

0.1/6.9   Rowe Well Road comes in from the left (southeast). You will return to this point at the end of the loop. Continue straight on Hermit Road and climb the hill. Just before the climb, if you walk a short distance toward the rim, you can find excellent examples of fossils in the limestone outcroppings near the hiking trail.

1.1/5.9   Trailview Overlook is the first bus stop you reach. Take the short walk to the overlook for an excellent view of the Bright Angel Trail, Grand Canyon Village, and the San Francisco Peaks in the distance.

Mile

1.7/5.3   Here you pass Maricopa Point.

2.2/4.8   The concrete structure near the rim is the Powell Memorial. Climb its steps for views of the Orphan Mine and Horn Creek.

2.4/4.6   Hopi Point, a favorite place to watch the sunset, is the only stop along this ride route where eastbound buses will pick you up. A long section of the Colorado River, including a portion of Granite Rapids, is visible to the west.

3.2/3.8   Here you reach Mohave Point.

4.2/2.8   The Abyss gives you a dizzying look over the steep canyon walls. On the east side of The Abyss, the Great Mohave Wall drops 3,000 feet to the Tonto Plateau below. At the bus stop information sign, look for a road that heads south into the piñon-juniper forest. Go left (south) around the gate onto the gravel road.

4.3/2.7   Stay left and take the gravel road that goes under the powerline.

4.5/2.5   At the fork in the road, go left (southeast) along the power-line. (The road to the right, signed as "W6A," goes to Rowe Well Picnic Area.) Then go over a berm and descend on a faint road into a forested drainage.

5.0/2.0   The old road joins a wider road that leads to a gravel pit. Continue south.

5.7/1.3   When you reach the gravel Rowe Well Road, turn left (northeast). This road is open to motorized vehicles, so watch for traffic as you begin a steady but gradual climb.

6.4/0.6   The road turns to pavement here. Ride past a side road that leads to the dog kennels.

6.7/0.3   The road to the right leads to the Maswik Lodge, in case you parked there. To get to the Village Route Transfer Stop, continue ahead.

6.8/0.2   Go around the gate.

6.9/0.1   At the stop sign, you are back on Hermit Road. Turn right.

7.0/0.0   Return to the Village Route Transfer Stop.

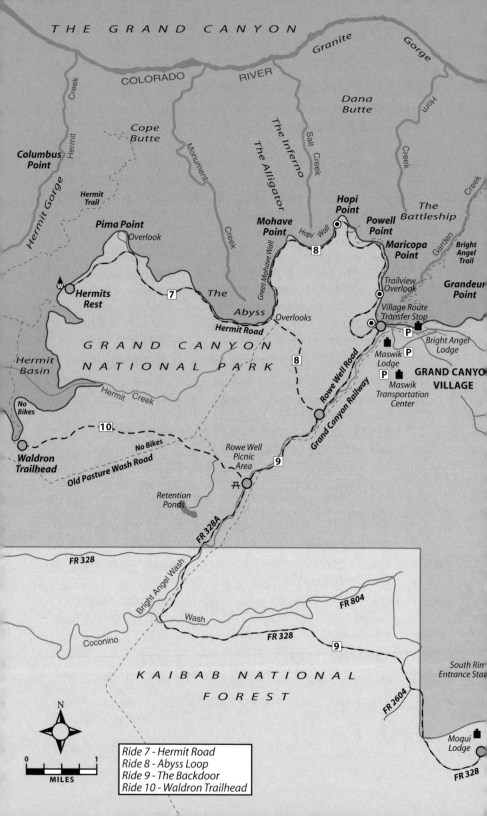

THE GRAND CANYON

COLORADO   RIVER   Granite   Gorge

Creek

Cope
Butte

Dana
Butte

Columbus
Point

Hermit Gorge

Hermit Trail

Monument

The Inferno

The Alligator

Salt Creek

Hopi
Point

The
Battleship

Creek

Bright
Angel
Trail

Pima Point

Overlook

Mohave
Point

Great Mohave Wall

Hopi Wall

Powell
Point

Maricopa
Point

Garden

Grandeur
Point

7

W Hermits
Rest

The

8

Trailview
Overlook

Abyss

Village Route
Transfer Stop

GRAND CANYON
NATIONAL PARK

Overlooks

Hermit Road

8

Bright Angel
Lodge

Maswik
Lodge

GRAND CANYON
VILLAGE

Hermit
Basin

No
Bikes

Hermit Creek

Rowe Well Road

Maswik
Transportation
Center

10

No Bikes

Old Pasture Wash Road

Waldron
Trailhead

Rowe Well
Picnic
Area

Grand Canyon Railway

9

Retention
Ponds

FR 328A

FR 328

FR 328

Bright Angel Wash

Wash

FR 804

FR 328

9

Coconino

South Rim
Entrance Sta.

KAIBAB   NATIONAL

FR 2604

FOREST

N

Moqui
Lodge

0   1

MILES   FR 328

Ride 7 - Hermit Road
Ride 8 - Abyss Loop
Ride 9 - The Backdoor
Ride 10 - Waldron Trailhead

Ride 9 **THE BACKDOOR**

Distance: 10.0 miles

Difficulty: Moderate

Technical Rating: Beginner

Type: Double-track/Road

Season
All year except when the road is
muddy or snow-covered.

Signage
Good.

Permits and Fees
$10–$20 for a seven-day park pass;
$40 for a pass good for a year.

Access to Trailhead
From the South Rim Entrance Station
of Grand Canyon National Park, drive
about 1 mile south on AZ 64. The
start of this route, Moqui Lodge, is on
the west side of the highway in the

*While biking this route, you might see
a train on the historic Grand Canyon
Railway.*

Kaibab National Forest. The route description begins on the south side
of the lodge, behind the gas station, at the start of FR 328.

Trail Overview
I call this ride The Backdoor because it is the "back way" into the park.
This route avoids the crowds and parking problems that often plague
motorists who drive in on the main park road, AZ 64. Early in the park's
history, Grand Canyon travelers used this road as an entrance to the park.
If you time your ride right, you might get to see the Grand Canyon train
chugging by on the railroad tracks.

Located in the Kaibab National Forest, the Moqui Lodge at the
start of the ride offers a restaurant, a gas station, and opportunities for
horseback riding. The route terminates inside the park at the Maswik
Lodge. Near the lodge is the Maswik Transportation Center, where you
can obtain backcountry permits or catch the free park shuttle buses to
other areas on the South Rim. Park buses do accommodate bikes on
their front-mounted racks, or you can bring a lock, leave your bike at
the bus station, and begin some park adventuring on foot.

Route Description

Mile

0.0/10.0   Head to the gravel FR 328 at the south end of Moqui Lodge, near the gas station. Follow the signs for Apache Stables and Pasture Wash.

0.4/9.6   Cross a cattle guard here. Stay straight ahead and go past the ranch.

1.0/9.0   Go under a powerline, then follow it along the park boundary.

1.8/8.2   Cross FR 2604 and FR 804. Begin a gradual climb that flattens out in about a mile.

4.1/5.9   Free primitive camping spots are available where a road curves in from the east. Stay on FR 328.

4.6/5.4   At the crest of the hill, admire the view of Mount Trumball before you descend.

5.0/5.0   Go right (northeast) onto Rowe Well Road at the intersection of FR 328 and FR 328A. Pasture Wash is 18 miles to the west if you're looking for a longer ride, but for Ride 9 stay right and follow the Grand Canyon Railway into the park.

5.6/4.4   Cross the railroad tracks, then go right (northeast) and cross a cattle guard.

5.7/4.3   Cross a dry stream, then climb along a drainage.

6.1/3.9   The route enters the park here when you cross the cattle guard.

Ride 9   **Total Elevation Gain:** 500 Feet
Total Elevation Loss: 350 Feet
Change in Elevation: 400 Feet

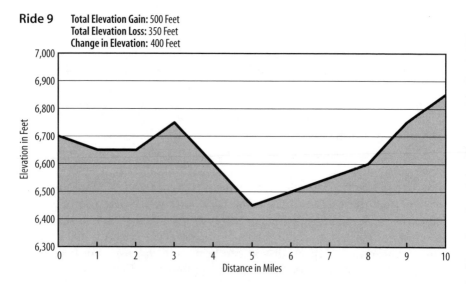

Mile

6.8/3.2   The grade levels out a bit as you continue to trace the railroad's path through a forest of ponderosa pines.

7.0/3.0   Look for the Rowe Well Picnic Area structure on your left (northwest). This used to be the site of Hamilton's Garage and Store in the 1930s.

7.3/2.7   Cross over to the southeast side of the tracks.

7.7/2.3   You can ride up this side road to the right (southeast) into a quiet, shallow canyon or continue straight ahead to the end of this ride.

8.0/2.0   Cross the railroad tracks again.

8.4/1.6   Reclaimed water makes the vegetation lush here, but the sign warns that the water in the stream is not safe for consumption. Be on the lookout for elk.

9.1/0.9   The road turns to pavement here. You soon pass two roads on your right (southeast). The first goes to the park kennels and the second leads to the Maswik Lodge.

9.4/0.6   Just before the gate, turn onto the second road to the right (south). Cross the railroad tracks and then pass the laundry facility at the back of the lodge.

10.0/0.0   At the second stop sign, you see the Maswik Transportation Center across the railroad tracks. Go left to the parking area and the end of this ride.

At the Backcountry Information Center, you can inquire about biking and camping in the park's remote areas.

Ride 10 ▶ WALDRON TRAILHEAD

See map, p. 66.

Distance: 3.1 miles

Difficulty: Moderate

Technical Rating: Intermediate

Type: Double-track/Road

Season
All year except when the road is muddy or covered with snow.

Signage
Poor.

Permits and Fees
$10–$20 for a seven-day park pass; $40 for a pass good for a year.

The Waldron Trail was one of the first trails built in the area.

Access to Trailhead
To reach Rowe Well Picnic Area and the start of this ride, you can follow the directions given in Ride 9: The Backdoor (see p. 67), but the easiest approach is from inside the park. From the Maswik Lodge, take the road south (on the back side) of the lodge that leads to the park kennels. Cross the railroad tracks. When you come to a T intersection with Rowe Well Road, go left (southwest) and continue to follow the signs to the kennels. When you reach the side road to the kennels, continue straight along the northwest side of the railroad tracks. The paved road will become gravel. Rowe Well Picnic Area is on the right (northwest) side of the road, 2.1 miles from where the pavement ended.

Trail Overview
Experienced mountain bikers won't find this short ride too difficult, but it does involve a rocky ascent on the way back. A 4.0-mile (one way) hike to a scenic grotto with a year-round spring starts at the Waldron Trailhead, the ride's end. Built in the late 1800s, the Waldron Trail was one of the first trails to access Dripping Springs and Hermit Basin. A herd of elk hangs out in this area, so you might get lucky and see some of these majestic animals.

Route Description

Mile

0.0/3.1 From the shelter at Rowe Well Picnic Area, take the higher road to the northwest. The primitive road climbs along the edge of a small canyon through a scenic forest.

0.4/2.7 After the terrain levels out, the primitive road comes to a fork. Bear right (northeast). The fork to the left leads to some retention ponds.

0.5/2.6 At this next fork, head left (north).

1.0/2.1 Cross a double-track trail signed for foot traffic only. Then continue straight ahead on a primitive road through piñon-juniper forest. The road descends for the next 2.0 miles.

2.7/0.4 This rocky section is fun for intermediate bikers, but remember that you have to climb it on the way back. The trail switchbacks as it skirts the edge of a limestone canyon.

3.1/0.0 Bikers should stop here at the trailhead sign. The Waldron Trail starts to the right of the sign and enters a shallow drainage. From the Waldron Trailhead you can hike 4.0 miles to Dripping Springs, but be sure to save some energy for the climb back out.

Ride 10 Total Elevation Gain: 100 Feet
Total Elevation Loss: 250 Feet
Change in Elevation: 250 Feet

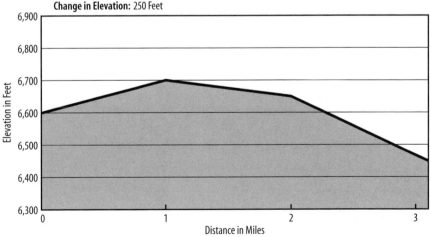

Ride 11 ▶ *VISHNU OVERLOOK LOOP*
See map, p. 75.

Vishnu Temple is the pointed butte in the background of this photograph, just left of center.

 This challenging but short ride makes a good introduction to mountain biking for older kids.

Distance: 1.5 miles

Difficulty: Easy

Technical Rating: Intermediate

Type: Single-track/Trail

Season
All year except when the trail is muddy or covered with snow.

Signage
Good.

Permits and Fees
$10–$20 for a seven-day park pass; $40 for a pass good for a year. Free access to the trailhead via FR 302.

Access to Trailhead

There are two ways to access Grandview Lookout, the ride's starting point. From Grand Canyon Village (South Rim Village), take Desert View Drive (AZ 64) east toward Desert View. About 2.0 miles southeast of the Grandview Point turnoff, take FR 310 south for 1.3 miles to the Grandview Lookout parking area. A pit toilet and trash can are available, but there is no water.

Alternately, you can avoid paying the park fee by reaching the trailhead via FR 302. On AZ 64 just south of Tusayan and 0.8 mile north of the airport entrance, take FR 302 northeast and follow the signs for 16.0 miles to Grandview Lookout. Two-wheel-drive vehicles can easily travel this gravel road, except during muddy conditions. Several primitive camping spots exist in the area.

The 80-foot-tall Grandview Lookout Tower was built in 1936.

Trail Overview

The Civilian Conservation Corps built the 80-foot-tall steel structure known as Grandview Lookout Tower in 1936. During periods of high fire danger, the U.S. Forest Service still assigns workers to staff the lookout. Be sure to climb the stairs high enough above the trees to see the view of the canyon.

The Vishnu Overlook is named after the butte to its northeast (just south of the North Rim). Vishnu Temple is one of the many buttes named by geologist Clarence Dutton, who surveyed the park for the U.S. government in 1880. Dutton's interest in Eastern religions is evident in the many "temples" he named after Hindu gods. Dutton thought the 7,533-foot-high Vishnu Temple looked like an Oriental pagoda. Vishnu, The Preserver of the Universe, is the Hindu god who looks after all creation.

Intermediate mountain bikers enjoy the tight switchbacks and numerous water bars on the Vishnu Trail. The distance is short enough that beginners should find the canyon view at the end well worth the technical challenges encountered during the ride.

Route Description

Mile

0.0/1.5   From the Grandview Lookout Trailhead, go under the fire tower. Follow the signs for the Vishnu Trail as it heads northeast between the fire tower and the cabin.

0.3/1.2   Take a moment to enjoy two nice views from the Coconino Rim (the second is the best).

0.4/1.1   At the T intersection, ride or walk to the left (northeast) to access the Vishnu Overlook.

0.7/0.8   After you go through the hiker gate, you come to a peaceful overlook with a bench—a nice place for a snack or lunch. Vishnu Temple is the pyramid-shaped butte to the northeast. Head back the way you came.

1.1/0.4   Back at the T intersection, continue straight (southwest) this time. Follow the sign that says "Return."

1.5/0.0   You're back at the Grandview Lookout Trailhead.

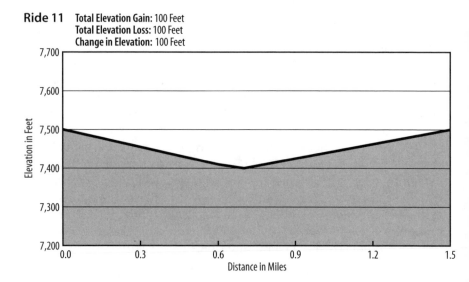

Ride 11   Total Elevation Gain: 100 Feet
Total Elevation Loss: 100 Feet
Change in Elevation: 100 Feet

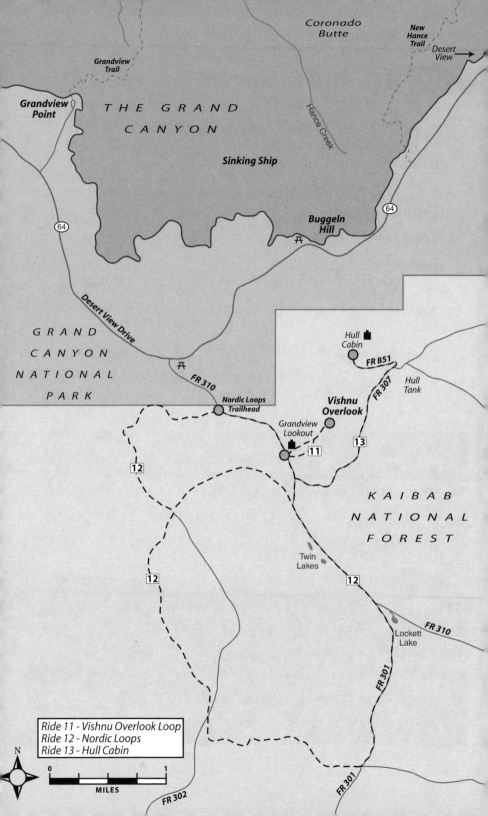

Coronado Butte

New Hance Trail

Desert View →

Grandview Trail

Grandview Point

THE GRAND CANYON

Hance Creek

Sinking Ship

64

Buggeln Hill

64

Desert View Drive

FR 310

GRAND CANYON NATIONAL PARK

Hull Cabin

FR 851

Hull Tank

Nordic Loops Trailhead

Vishnu Overlook

FR 307

Grandview Lookout

11

13

12

KAIBAB NATIONAL FOREST

Twin Lakes

12

FR 310

12

Lockett Lake

FR 301

FR 301

Ride 11 - Vishnu Overlook Loop
Ride 12 - Nordic Loops
Ride 13 - Hull Cabin

N

0   MILES   1

FR 302

Ride 12 **NORDIC LOOPS**
See map, p. 75.

Older kids should enjoy this pleasant route.

Distance: 3.7 to 8.8 miles

Difficulty: Moderate

Technical Rating: Beginner

Type: Double-track/Road

Season
All year except when the route is muddy or covered with snow.

Signage
Good.

Permits and Fees
$10–$20 for a seven-day park pass; $40 for a pass good for a year.
Free access to the trailhead via FR 302.

The world's largest ponderosa pine forest covers the Coconino Plateau.

Access to Trailhead

There are two ways to access Grandview Lookout, the ride's starting point. From Grand Canyon Village (South Rim Village), take Desert View Drive (AZ 64) east toward Desert View. About 2.0 miles southeast of the Grandview Point turnoff, take FR 310 south for 1.3 miles to the Grandview Lookout parking area. A pit toilet and trash can are available, but there is no water.

Alternately, you can avoid paying the park fee by reaching the trailhead via FR 302. On AZ 64 just south of Tusayan and 0.8 mile north of the airport entrance, take FR 302 northeast and follow the signs for 16.0 miles to Grandview Lookout. Two-wheel-drive vehicles can easily travel this gravel road, except during muddy conditions. Several primitive camping spots exist in the area.

Trail Overview

The Forest Service built these trails for Nordic skiers, but bikers can use these routes when there's no snow. The trails are marked with brown Carsonite posts featuring a sticker of a skier. Quiet riding, elk sightings, open meadows, and exposed limestone outcroppings are some of the highlights of this pleasant route.

Route Description

Mile

0.0/8.8   From the Grandview Lookout Trailhead, go north on FR 310.

0.6/8.2   Turn left (west) at the Nordic Trails sign. Study the map and sign the logbook before you take the easy grade that travels through the forest along the park boundary.

1.2/7.6   Notice the ski trail going cross-country here. Stay on the road because the trail soon reconnects.

1.4/7.4   Stay straight when you pass the quarry on your right (west).

1.6/7.2   Follow the skier signs through this area. The trail bends back to the left (east).

2.2/6.6   After an easy ride through a meadow, continue straight ahead on the trail. Ignore the road that comes in from the west.

2.5/6.3   At the T intersection, posts mark Trail A in both directions. For the short loop, go left (northeast) here, then take FR 310 left (north) to return to Grandview Lookout Trailhead. For the longer loop described here, go right (southwest) and immediately roll over a dirt berm.

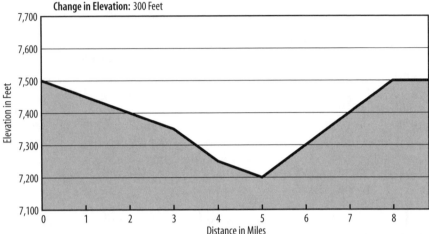

Ride 12   Total Elevation Gain: 300 Feet
Total Elevation Loss: 300 Feet
Change in Elevation: 300 Feet

Mile

3.5/5.3   Isn't this fun? A pleasant downhill coast through a serene meadow allows time for sightseeing. Look for elk and purple lupine during the summer. Take note of the exposed limestone cliffs and the impressive ponderosa pines.

4.5/4.3   Turn left (east) onto a faint double track that climbs gradually at first.

5.9/2.9   At the four-way intersection, go left (northeast) on gravel FR 301. Continue to make up for that fun descent by climbing gradually for the next mile.

7.4/1.4   At the T intersection with FR 310, go left (north). The grade levels out somewhat.

8.1/0.7   Twin Lakes are on the left (west) side of the road. These lakes are dry during drought years.

8.7/0.1   At this intersection, continue straight ahead (north). This is where the shortcut loop at mile 2.5 rejoins the route. Just ahead, FR 307 comes in from the right (east). This is the road that leads to Hull Cabin (see Ride 13, opposite).

8.8/0.0   Return to Grandview Lookout Trailhead.

Ride 13 ▸ HULL CABIN
See map, p. 75.

The trailhead at Grandview Lookout is a hub for many biking opportunities.

Distance: 2.0 miles

Difficulty: Moderate

Technical Rating: Beginner

Type: Double-track/Road

Season
All year except when the route is muddy or covered with snow.

Signage
Good.

Permits and Fees
$10–$20 for a seven-day park pass; $40 for a pass good for a year.
Free access to the trailhead via FR 302.

Access to Trailhead
There are two ways to access Grandview Lookout, the ride's starting
point. From Grand Canyon Village (South Rim Village), take Desert View

Drive (AZ 64) east toward Desert View. About 2.0 miles southeast of the Grandview Point turnoff, take FR 310 south for 1.3 miles to the Grandview Lookout parking area. A pit toilet and trash can are available, but there is no water.

Alternately, you can avoid paying the park fee by reaching the trailhead via FR 302. On AZ 64 just south of Tusayan and 0.8 mile north of the airport entrance, take FR 302 northeast and follow the signs for 16.0 miles to Grandview Lookout. Two-wheel-drive vehicles can easily travel this gravel road, except during muddy conditions. Several primitive camping spots exist in the area.

Trail Overview

This short ride involves a steep descent, which becomes a steep climb on the return trip—but the views of the Coconino Rim on the way down to historic Hull Cabin make the effort worthwhile. The residential Hull Cabin is part of the Hull Cabin Historic District, which also includes a storage cabin, a barn, and a water tank. This area was established by the Hull brothers, sheep ranchers who began to build here in 1888. In 1907, the U.S. Forest Service acquired the cabin for use as a ranger station. Even today, you might see seasonal crews using these facilities as a temporary home.

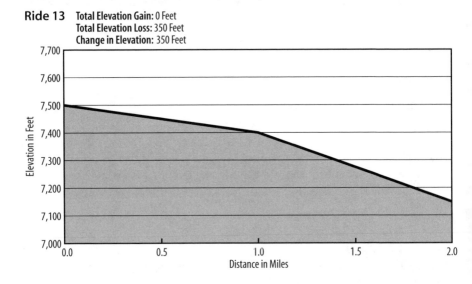

Ride 13   Total Elevation Gain: 0 Feet
Total Elevation Loss: 350 Feet
Change in Elevation: 350 Feet

Route Description

Mile

0.0/2.0   From the Grandview Lookout Trailhead, go south on FR 310.

0.1/1.9   Turn left (east) on FR 307. Follow the signs to Hull Cabin.

0.4/1.6   After you roll over a cattle guard, look for where the Arizona Trail crosses the road.

0.8/1.2   On the descent, enjoy views of the Grand Canyon through the trees. The road continues to descend along a steep, forested canyon.

1.4/0.6   Near the bottom of the descent, you pass by Hull Tank.

1.6/0.4   The route to Hull Cabin exits FR 307 at a switchback that takes you left (west) onto FR 851. Follow the signs to stay on track. Go through a gate and then continue west on an easy grade.

2.0/0.0   A Forest Service sign explains the history of Hull Cabin. Spend some time exploring the grounds before you take on that tough climb back to the trailhead.

The sheep-ranching Hull brothers built Hull Cabin in the late 1800s.

Ride 14 ▸ *COCONINO RIM LOOP*
See map, p. 84.

Distance: 14.2 miles

Difficulty: Moderate

Technical Rating: Intermediate

Type: Single-track/Trail
and Double-track/Road

Season
All year except when the route is
muddy or covered with snow.

Signage
Good.

Permits and Fees
$10–$20 for a seven-day park
pass; $40 for a pass good for a
year. Free access to the trailhead
via FR 302.

Access to Trailhead
There are two ways to access
Grandview Lookout, the ride's
starting point. From Grand
Canyon Village (South Rim
Village), take Desert View Drive

*The Coconino Rim Loop starts with a
short, self-guided nature tour.*

(AZ 64) east toward Desert View. About 2.0 miles southeast of the
Grandview Point turnoff, take FR 310 south for 1.3 miles to the Grandview
Lookout parking area. A pit toilet and trash can are available, but there
is no water. The trail starts behind the Arizona Trail display sign.

Alternately, you can avoid paying the park fee by reaching the
trailhead via FR 302. On AZ 64 just south of Tusayan and 0.8 mile
north of the airport entrance, take FR 302 northeast and follow the
signs for 16.0 miles to Grandview Lookout. Two-wheel-drive vehicles
can easily travel this gravel road, except during muddy conditions.
Several primitive camping spots exist in the area.

Trail Overview

This loop incorporates one of the best sections of the Arizona Trail (AZT) for mountain biking. The Coconino Rim section of the AZT includes a short, self-guided nature path with interpretive displays about the natural history of dwarf mistletoe, views of the Grand Canyon and Painted Desert, and an excellent chance for elk encounters.

I've rated this ride as moderate/intermediate, but it's a nice day loop for beginners willing to try some single track. Bring water and some snacks and take the time to make a fun day of it. If this section of the AZT gets you dreaming of riding the whole thing all the way to Mexico, check into my other book, *Biking the Arizona Trail: The Complete Guide to Day-Riding and Thru-Biking* (see Appendix D).

Route Description

Mile

0.0/14.2   Go under the AZT sign onto a gravel nature path. The wooden sign indicates this is the Coconino Rim section of the AZT.

0.2/14.0   At the "Will mistletoe be wiped out?" sign, leave the nature trail by taking the dirt path to the left (east).

0.3/13.9   Cross FR 307.

1.9/12.3   Look for a nice view to the east as you ride through a clearing. An interpretive sign informs you that a dwarf mistletoe infestation wiped out the forest that once covered this area.

2.9/11.3   This primitive campsite (no water) offers a sunrise view over the Coconino Rim.

3.3/10.9   Here are more primitive campsites with fine vistas. Take in the route's best view of the Painted Desert.

6.5/7.7   Pass through the first of many cattle gates.

7.3/6.9   Travel over a series of short, steep sections.

8.3/5.9   Take the double track to the right (west), as the signs direct. This is a bike detour around steep switchbacks.

8.4/5.8   At the wooden sign, the AZT continues to the left (south). Keep to the Coconino Rim Loop by going straight on the faint road. Follow the directions on the sign for "G.V. Return," which will lead you back to Grandview Lookout Trailhead via Coconino Rim Road (FR 310).

8.5/5.7   At the road, another sign shows you the way. Go right (north) on FR 310. The route follows a mostly uphill grade.

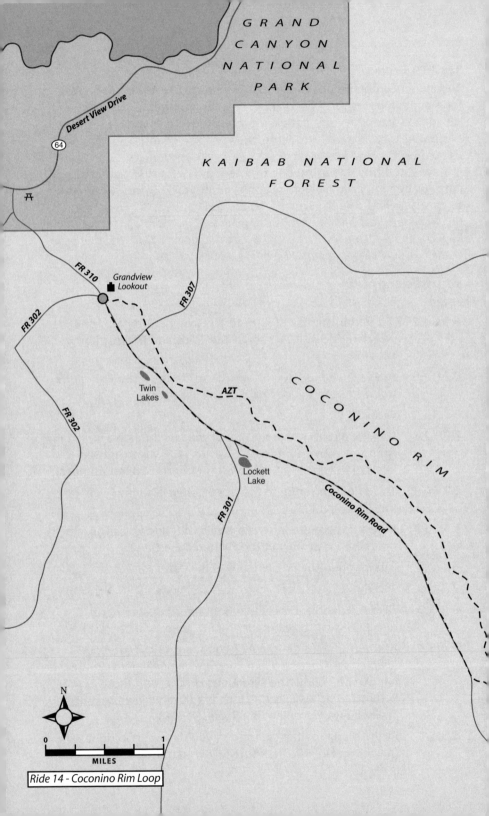

GRAND
CANYON
NATIONAL
PARK

Desert View Drive

64

KAIBAB NATIONAL
FOREST

FR 310

Grandview
Lookout

FR 307

FR 302

FR 302

Twin
Lakes

AZT

COCONINO RIM

Lockett
Lake

FR 301

Coconino Rim Road

N

0   1
MILES

Ride 14 - Coconino Rim Loop

Ride 14 Total Elevation Gain: 250 Feet
Total Elevation Loss: 250 Feet
Change in Elevation: 250 Feet

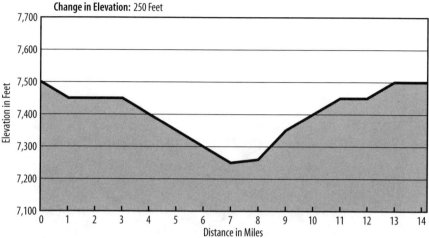

Mile

9.6/4.6   You cross a cattle guard here.

10.2/4.0   There is a concrete basin on the right (northeast).

12.5/1.7   The short spur to Lockett Lake is on your left (southwest).

12.7/1.5   This is the intersection with FR 301 and the Nordic Loops (see Ride 12, p. 76). Stay north on FR 310.

13.5/0.7   Twin Lakes are on your left (west). Don't expect any water during drought years.

14.2/0.0   Return to the Grandview Lookout Trailhead.

Ride 15 ► RED BUTTE LOOP

See map, p. 89.

The Havasupai name for Red Butte means "mountain of the clenched fist."

Distance: 8.9 miles

Difficulty: Moderate

Technical Rating: Beginner

Type: Double-track/Road

Season
All year except when the road is muddy or covered with snow.

Signage
Fair.

Access to Trailhead
From the Grand Canyon's South Rim Entrance Station, drive south on AZ 64 to mile marker 224. Just north of the Kaibab National Forest boundary, take the signed FR 320 to the left (east). Drive 1.5 miles to the intersection with FR 340 and turn left (north). Follow FR 340 for 1.0 mile to FR 340A. Go right (east) on FR 340A for 0.3 mile to the Red Butte Trailhead.

Trail Overview

This loop ride makes a circuit around the 7,326-foot-high geologic formation of Red Butte, which the Havasupai tribe calls "Hue-ga-da-wi-za," mountain of the clenched fist. The short hike to the top of the butte leads to a USFS lookout tower with a unique view of the Grand Canyon.

Red Butte is an example of the soft mudstone formations that once covered this entire portion of the Colorado Plateau. A cap of basalt, a hard volcanic rock, has protected Red Butte from the erosional forces that have washed away the surrounding soil, leaving the butte behind as a lonesome reminder of what used to be.

The area around Red Butte is a good example of piñon-juniper forests intermixed with sagebrush plains. Look for elk in the cooler months. If you're lucky, you might get treated to a pronghorn antelope sighting.

Ride 15 Total Elevation Gain: 250 Feet
Total Elevation Loss: 250 Feet
Change in Elevation: 250 Feet

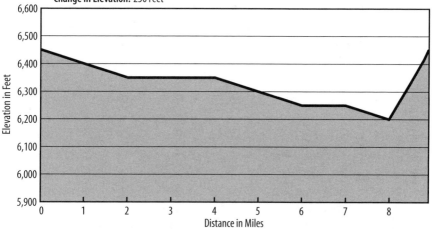

Route Description

Mile

0.0/8.9   From the Red Butte Trailhead, ride back down FR 340A, then turn right (north) onto FR 340.

0.4/8.5   Stay north on FR 340, passing several minor roads as you travel through sagebrush plains.

1.6/7.3   Climb a little hill as you make your way to the intersection with FR 305 (you'll see a metal water tank). Go right (east) on FR 305. Look for the fire tower on top of Red Butte.

Mile

2.7/6.2	Where another forest road comes in, stay straight and begin a gradual climb.
3.0/5.9	Pass two roads that head south toward the butte. Views of the San Francisco Peaks open up to the southeast.
4.0/4.9	An even better view of the peaks lies ahead as you descend. When I did this route, I saw three trophy elk cross the road here.
4.8/4.1	Stay on FR 305 as the road bends to the south. Look west to see the exposed gray rock on Red Butte. This is the "lava cap" that has protected the butte from erosion. Just past Curley Wallace Tank, the road turns into the gravel FR 320.
5.7/3.2	Climb gradually as you head west.
7.0/1.9	Red Butte Tank is to your right (north).
7.6/1.3	Turn right (north) onto the red dirt FR 340 and make your way back to the west side of Red Butte.
8.6/0.3	Take FR 340A right (east).
8.9/0.0	Finish the loop at Red Butte Trailhead.

Red Butte, viewed here from the north, is the centerpiece of this loop ride.

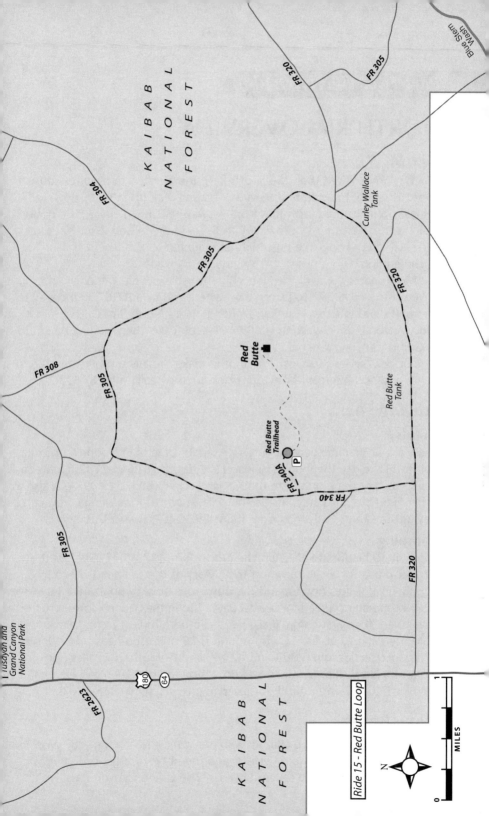

Tusayan and
Grand Canyon
National Park

KAIBAB NATIONAL FOREST

FR 2623

180
64

KAIBAB
NATIONAL
FOREST

FR 305

FR 308

FR 305

FR 304

FR 305

FR 305

FR 320

FR 305

Blue Stem
Wash

Curley Wallace
Tank

FR 320

Red Butte Tank

FR 320

Red
Butte

Red Butte
Trailhead

FR 340A

FR 340

P

Ride 15 - Red Butte Loop

N

MILES

0   1

Part Two: The North Rim

NORTH RIM OVERVIEW

Getting There

Much more isolated than the South Rim, the North Rim requires some effort to reach. In addition, heavy winter snowfall often shuts down all vehicle traffic to the North Rim from November to early June. The good news is the North Rim's proximity to Bryce Canyon and Zion National Parks, which provides the possibility of planning a "Grand Circle Tour" of all three parks.

Most people come to the North Rim by vehicle. From Fredonia, Arizona, drive south on US 89A to Jacob Lake, where you take AZ 67 all the way to the road's end in Grand Canyon National Park's North Rim District. From Page, Arizona, drive west on US 89A to Jacob Lake, then take AZ 67 south to Grand Canyon National Park.

For bus service, Transcanyon Shuttle makes a daily trip between the North and South Rims. Make your reservation by calling (928) 638-2820.

Staying There

Hotels

There are several inexpensive hotels in Kanab, Utah, and Fredonia, Arizona. In Jacob Lake, try the lodge at Jacob Lake Inn, (520) 643-7232. Eighteen miles north of the North Rim, the Kaibab Lodge, (800) 525-0924, is also a convenient place to stay. Inside the park at North Rim Village, you can stay at the Grand Canyon Lodge, (888) 297-2757, www.nps.gov/grca/.

Camping

The Kaibab National Forest on the North Rim, (928) 643-7395, is the perfect place for a car-camping trip. Most of the trailheads have free primitive campsites nearby, and the numerous biking opportunities can easily keep you occupied for several days. Also in the national forest are the developed (fee), first-come, first-served campgrounds at Jacob Lake and DeMotte Park. Jacob Lake Campground is 30 miles southeast of Fredonia at the intersection of US 89A and AZ 67, and DeMotte is 7 miles north of the park's North Rim Entrance Station. Inside the park, you can camp at the North Rim Campground; for reservations, call (800) 365-2267.

Day-Use Fees

The National Park Service charges $20 per vehicle for a seven-day pass. Pedestrians, bicyclists, motorcyclists, and members of organized groups pay $10 per person for a seven-day pass. The Grand Canyon Pass, which grants unlimited park access for a year, is $40. Currently, there is no day-use fee for national forest lands.

Food, Supplies, and Other Amenities

Jacob Lake, DeMotte Park, and North Rim Village all offer restaurants. Jacob Lake Inn sells home-baked goodies that you won't have to feel guilty about eating after a hard day's ride. Limited groceries, as well as shower and laundry facilities, are available at Jacob Lake and North Rim Village. The bike stores nearest the North Rim are in St. George, Utah, and Page, Arizona (see Appendix B).

Information

If you need more information while you are in the area, you can stop by one of these places:

• North Kaibab Ranger District Office, Kaibab National Forest (USFS): 430 S. Main, Fredonia, (928) 643-7395, www.fs.fed.us/r3/kai/.

• Kaibab Plateau Visitor Center (USFS/NPS): In Jacob Lake, west of AZ 67 next to Jacob Lake Inn, (928) 643-7298 (see North Rim Overview map, p. 92).

• North Rim Visitor Center (NPS): At the end of AZ 67 near Grand Canyon Lodge, www.nps.gov/grca (see North Rim Overview map, p. 92).

• North Rim Backcountry Information Center (NPS): At the North Rim Ranger Station, west of AZ 67 and north of the Grand Canyon Lodge, (928) 638-7875, www.nps.gov/grca/backcountry/ (see North Rim Overview map, p. 92).

The Grand Staircase

While on the Kaibab Plateau, you are, in a geologic sense, on the bottom step of The Grand Staircase. The Grand Staircase is a series of four cliffs that drop down from Bryce Canyon to the North Rim of the Grand Canyon. From the north, the Pink Cliffs of Bryce Canyon National Park rise above the White Cliffs of Zion National Park. The White Cliffs lead to the Gray Cliffs, which step down to the Vermilion Cliffs. The Kaibab Plateau lies at the bottom of the "staircase."

On clear days, you can see a portion of the Grand Staircase from several spots on the North Rim (Marble View Overlook and East Rim View). Look for the cliffs rising above the Colorado Plateau like a set of gigantic stairs suitable for the likes of Paul Bunyan. If you have the time, consider taking the Grand Circle Tour, a trip that takes in all three national parks. There are biking trails at Zion and Bryce Canyon National Parks, as well.

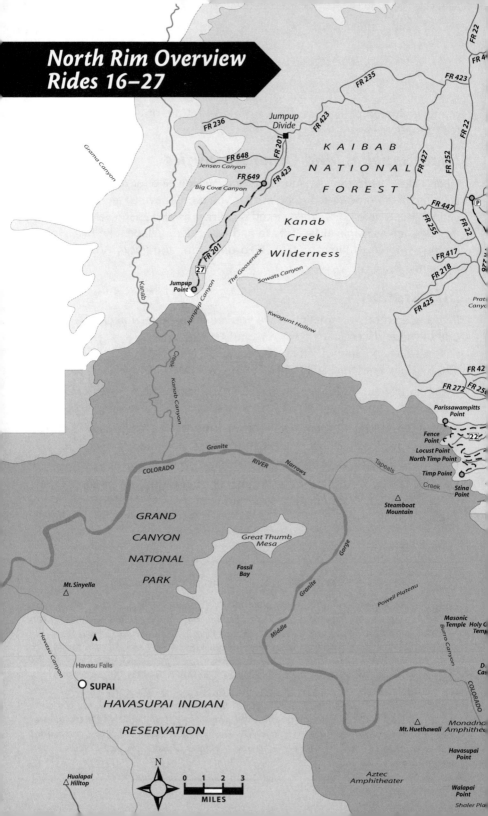

North Rim Overview
Rides 16–27

KAIBAB NATIONAL FOREST

FR 22
FR 4
FR 423
FR 235
FR 236
Jumpup Divide
FR 423
FR 22
FR 201
FR 648
Jensen Canyon
FR 427
FR 252
FR 649
FR 423
Big Cove Canyon
FR 447
FR 255
FR 22
Kanab Creek Wilderness
FR 417
FR 218
FR 201
27
The Gooseneck
Sowats Canyon
FR 425
Prat Canyon
Jumpup Point
Kwagunt Hollow
Grama Canyon

Kanab
Jumpup Canyon
Creek
Kanab Canyon
FR 42
FR 272
FR 256
Parissawampitts Point
Fence Point
22
Granite
Locust Point
North Timp Point
RIVER
Narrows
Tapeats
Timp Point
COLORADO
Creek
Stina Point
Steamboat Mountain

GRAND CANYON NATIONAL PARK
Great Thumb Mesa
Gorge
Granite
Fossil Bay
Powell Plateau
Mt. Sinyella
Middle
Masonic Temple Holy G Temp
Burro Canyon
Havasu Canyon
D Cas
COLORADO
Havasu Falls
SUPAI
Mt. Huethawali
Monadno Amphithe
HAVASUPAI INDIAN RESERVATION
Havasupai Point
Hualapai Hilltop
N
0 1 2 3
MILES
Aztec Amphitheater
Walapai Point
Shaler Pla

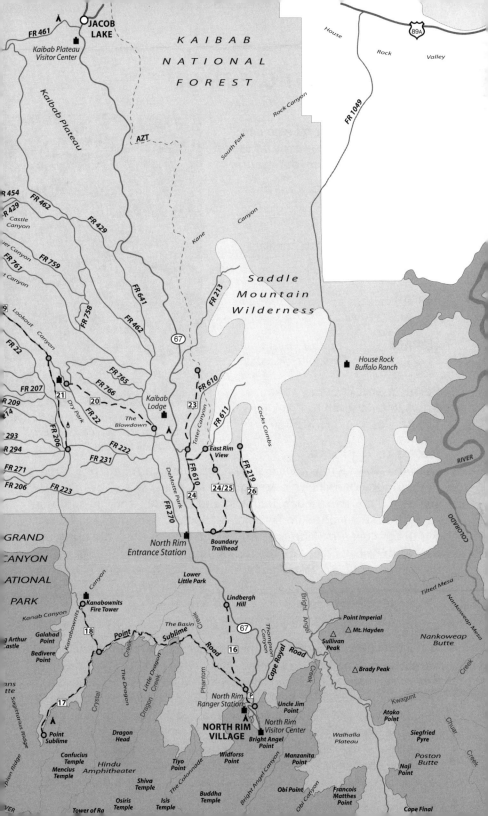

Ride 16 ▶ **MULTI-USE TRAIL**
See map, p. 96.

It's important to stay hydrated at the Grand Canyon, even on its cooler North and South Rims

🕺 *Teen-agers who can handle geared bikes will love the coast from north to south.*

Distance: 6.1 miles

Difficulty: Moderate

Technical Rating: Intermediate

Type: Single-track/Trail

Season
May to October.

Signage
Fair: Stickers on Carsonite posts.

Permits and Fees
$10–$20 for a seven-day park pass;
$40 for a pass good for a year.

Access to Trailhead
From the North Rim Entrance Station, go south on AZ 67 for 3.8 miles to the Lindbergh Hill Picnic Area on the left (east) side of the highway. To reach the North Kaibab Trailhead and the ride's end, go south on AZ 67 from the North Rim Entrance Station. After 11.0 miles, you will see the trailhead parking area on the left side of the highway. From the North Kaibab Trailhead, the turnoff for the Widforss Trailhead is 0.5 mile north on AZ 67. Take the dirt road that heads west and north from the turnoff at AZ 67 for a short distance to the Widforss Trailhead parking lot. Both trailheads are well signed.

Trail Overview
At the time of printing, the National Park Service had not yet established the official Arizona Trail (AZT) route through the park. The ride described here is one of the routes being considered. Although you might see signs designating this route as the AZT, the NPS currently calls it the Multi-Use Trail. Note that the NPS does not allow mountain biking on most park trails. The Multi-Use Trail is one of the few exceptions. Please abide by all park rules and regulations and yield to other trail users while on this route.

If you bike north to south, you will enjoy some fast riding on the way to where the North Kaibab Trail leads hikers off the rim and down into the depths of the Grand Canyon. Riding the hill up and out of Harvey Meadow makes northbound travel much more strenuous. I recommend that you start at Lindbergh Hill Picnic Area and have vehicle support meet you at either the North Kaibab or the Widforss Trailhead.

Ride 16 Total Elevation Gain: 100 Feet
Total Elevation Loss: 700 Feet
Change in Elevation: 700 Feet

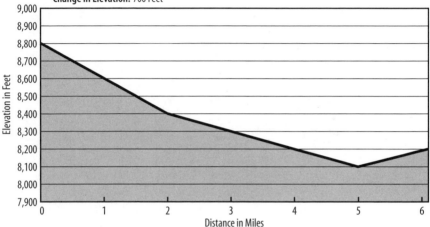

Route Description

Mile

0.0/6.1   From the paved pullout at the Lindbergh Hill Picnic Area, look for the signed trail that goes into the forest on the west side of AZ 67.

3.9/2.2   Enjoy a yahoo-fun gradual descent through aspen and pine trees. Pass through an area that has been burned to a crisp by a forest fire.

4.6/1.5   Cross the road before making a steep descent. (This is a steep climb for northbounders.)

4.9/1.2   At the bottom of the long descent, you reach Harvey Meadow. Turn left (south) on a dirt road and follow the signs to keep on track.

5.3/0.8   The Widforss Trailhead parking lot has a restroom.

5.6/0.5   Leave the dirt road for a primitive road (which is now a trail) that ascends to the right (south).

6.1/0.0   The trail jumps onto AZ 67. Watch for vehicle traffic as you cross the highway to reach the North Kaibab Trail parking lot. A water fountain is hidden behind some evergreens to the east of the trailhead sign.

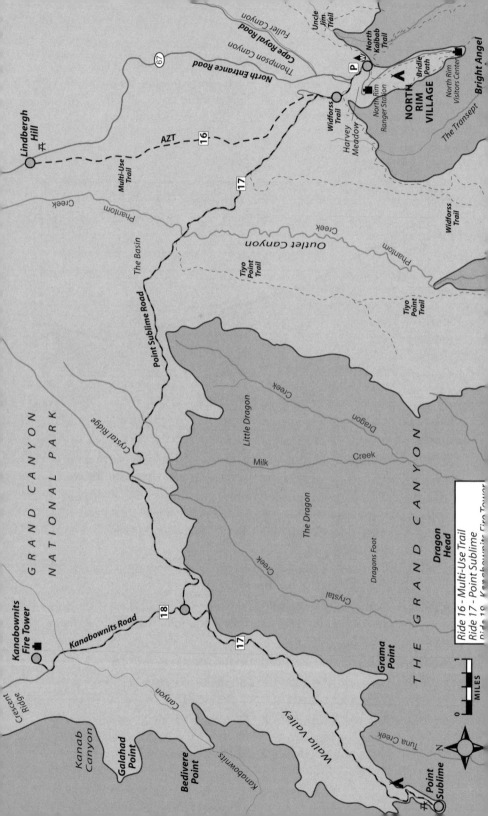

Ride 17 ▶ *POINT SUBLIME*

The phenomenal canyon view from Point Sublime demonstrates how it earned such a name.

Distance: 17.8 miles

Difficulty: Strenuous

Technical Rating: Intermediate

Type: Double-track/Road

Season
May to October.

Maps
Trails Illustrated: Grand Canyon National Park

Signage
Fair: Wooden signs.

Permits and Fees
$10–$20 for a seven-day park pass; $40 for a pass good for a year. Permits, available from the North Rim Backcountry Information Center (see North Rim Overview, p. 91), are required for overnight use only. Because of the area's popularity, it's best to reserve camping permits for Point Sublime well in advance of your trip.

Access to Trailhead

To get to the Widforss Trailhead from the North Kaibab Trailhead, drive north on AZ 67 for about 0.5 mile and turn left (west). Continue for another 0.5 mile to the parking area at Widforss Trailhead, where the route description starts. The road to this ride's end at Point Sublime is open to high-clearance vehicles. Overhead clearance is tight at times, which might pose a problem for riders who carry their bikes on their vehicle's roof.

Trail Overview

This challenging route leads to one of the best overlooks in the entire park. The panoramic view at the overlook will show you how Point Sublime earned its name. You can see rapids churning in the Colorado River below, and the sunset watching is top-notch.

If you bike the entire route, you'll work for those views at the end. Built in 1924, the dirt road to Point Sublime involves steep and plentiful roller-coaster hills for the first two-thirds of the route. The easiest way to do this ride is to have someone drop you off at mile 11.4 at the intersection with Kanabownits Road. From this dirt road, you can bike to the overlook on a 6.4-mile section of more flat terrain. You can also drive all the way to the overlook and ride the route backward from there.

Those who are lucky enough to get a camping permit can meet their vehicle support driver at the end of Point Sublime Road and camp for the night. Bikepackers can plan a challenging two-day mountain bike tour of the route. If you camp at Point Sublime, children could make short rides from the camping area. Whether you're out for an overnighter or just for the day, be sure to take plenty of water and supplies. This is a remote area with no facilities.

Ride 17 **Total Elevation Gain:** 650 Feet
Total Elevation Loss: 1,450 Feet
Change in Elevation: 1,000 Feet

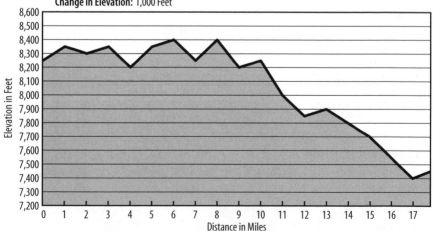

Route Description

Mile

0.0/17.8   From the Widforss Trailhead parking area, continue north on the dirt road.

0.3/17.5   Turn left (west) on Point Sublime Road. The Multi-Use Trail crosses the road here on its way north. Stay left on Point Sublime Road.

1.4/16.4   Stay right (north) on the most developed road.

1.9/15.9   The going gets steep as you begin some constant up-and-down riding.

3.6/14.2   The large meadow here is called The Basin. The road flattens out but gets sandy in spots. Several fire roads lead off the main route. These roads are closed to cyclists.

4.8/13.0   Leave the meadow as the road heads southwest into the forest.

5.1/12.7   Climb through an area scorched by forest fire and then climb some more. You get peek-a-boo views of the Grand Canyon as you skirt the rim of Dragon Creek Canyon.

6.5/11.3   Reach a small meadow. Look for wildflowers such as purple lupine and Indian paintbrush in the summer.

9.1/8.7   You get a little break from the climbing as the road flattens out under a shady forest before you begin a long descent.

10.9/6.9   At this intersection, stay right (north). A pullout to the left has a view of the canyon. Descend to the next intersection.

11.4/6.4   Follow signs to the left (south) to Point Sublime. The road to the right (north) is Kanabownits Road.

12.1/5.7   At first, the road is flat through this section. Then it makes a steep climb. After the climb, enjoy a more pleasant grade that offers occasional views of Crystal Creek Canyon before you begin a long, gradual descent through a shady pine forest.

16.6/1.2   A gradual climb gets steeper as you make a switchback up onto the peninsula that leads to Point Sublime.

16.9/0.9   Nice view, but you're not there yet. Keep climbing, and then grind out the last hill.

17.5/0.3   Pass two campsites with shaded picnic tables. A permit is required to camp here overnight.

Mile

17.8/0.0   Welcome to Point Sublime. Walk down the short path to an even better view. You can see some of the Colorado River's rapids, and on clear days the views stretch all the way across the Coconino Plateau to the San Francisco Peaks. You might spy tour helicopters traveling back and forth over the formation known as The Dragon. I don't find the helicopter noise to be as disturbing as some claim it to be. The helicopter tours stop before sunset.

The sweeping vistas at Point Sublime are a Grand Canyon biker's ultimate reward.

Burn, Baby, Burn

Evidence of forest fire exists in many places on the North Rim, as fires are a yearly occurrence on the Kaibab Plateau. Most people now realize that fires play an important role in the life cycle of a healthy forest ecosystem. Many plants such as quaking aspen actually flourish in scorched areas. Because of this phenomenon, the National Park Service and the Forest Service sometimes allow fires to burn, as long as people and structures are not in harm's way. However, when a forest fire poses a significant threat to safety, firefighters work aggressively to suppress it. During periods of drought or extreme fire danger, public lands managers might decide to close the forests to visitation in order to avoid human-caused fires. Particularly during the summer and early fall, it is a good idea to call the USFS (see Appendix C) before you visit to make sure the forest isn't closed.

Ride 18 ▶ KANABOWNITS FIRE TOWER

See map, p. 96.

Distance: 3.1 miles

Difficulty: Moderate

Technical Rating: Intermediate

Type: Double-track/Road

Season
May to October.

Signage
Poor: Wooden signs.

Permits and Fees
$10–$20 for a seven-day park pass; $40 for a pass good for a year. Permits, available from the North Rim Backcountry Information Center (see North Rim Overview, p. 91), are required for overnight use only. Request a camping permit for Point Sublime.

Kanabownits Road travels under the shady canopy of Boreal forest.

Access to Trailhead
From the North Kaibab Trailhead, drive north on AZ 67 for about 0.5 mile and then turn left (west) onto the road leading to the Widforss Trailhead. After you pass the trailhead, go left (northwest) on Point Sublime Road. (You can follow the route description for Ride 17: Point Sublime, p. 97.) After 11.4 miles, you reach the intersection with Kanabownits Road. The route description starts here. Mountain bikers starting from Point Sublime can add 6.0 miles (one way) to the ride by biking from the picnic area.

Note that the road to Point Sublime is open to high-clearance vehicles. The overhead clearance is tight at times, which might pose a problem for riders who carry their bikes on their vehicle's roof.

Trail Overview
This moderate but short ride takes you deep into the dark alpine forests of the North Rim. A steep climb to the Kanabownits Fire Tower awaits at the end. Climb the steps of the tower for a unique view of the canyon and the Kaibab Plateau. Kanabownits Road leads to other Forest Service roads that you can incorporate into a longer bike tour. Stock up on plenty of water and supplies before venturing into this isolated area.

Route Description

Mile

0.0/3.1   From the intersection of Kanabownits and Point Sublime Roads, go north on Kanabownits Road. The grade is gradual at first. Expect a few sandy spots.

1.1/2.0   At the top of a climb, you find a forest of large, old-growth ponderosa pines.

1.8/1.3   Continue to roll up and down over several hills.

2.4/0.7   Enjoy a nice grade through a lush meadow before you begin a 0.5-mile climb.

3.1/0.0   Top out at an intersection with a fire road to the right (northeast) that leads to the Kanabownits Fire Tower. Bike or hike the additional 0.4 mile to the tower, where you can climb up the stairs to get a view over the trees.

NOTE: From the tower, long-distance bikers can continue on Kanabownits Road for 7.2 miles to Forest Service roads that link up with the Rainbow Rim Trail (see Ride 22, p. 112.) Biking out to Fire Point and Swamp Point just south of the Rainbow Rim Trail are also options for hardy mountain bikers who want to explore isolated and rarely seen overlooks. Contact the North Rim Backcountry Information Center (see p. 91) for more information.

Ride 18   **Total Elevation Gain:** 500 Feet
Total Elevation Loss: 100 Feet
Change in Elevation: 400 Feet

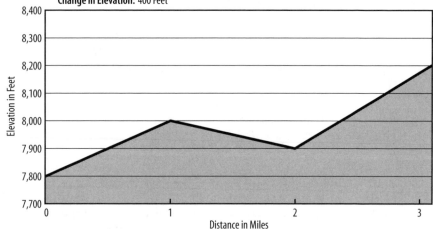

Ride 19 ▶ *LOOKOUT CANYON*

See map, p. 106.

This ride is great for older kids on geared bikes, especially if you do a shuttle so they can ride the mostly downhill grade going from south to north.

Distance: 11.5 miles

Difficulty: Moderate

Technical Rating: Beginner

Type: Double-track/Trail

Season
May to October.

Signage
Good: USFS markers on Carsonite posts and wooden signs.

You can access several Forest Service trails from Dry Park.

Water Sources
Inside the corral at mile 9.4, there is a stock tank fed by Riggs Springs.

Access to Trailhead
To access the ride's south end, go south from Jacob Lake Inn on AZ 67 for 26.5 miles to FR 22 at DeMotte Park. Go right (west) on FR 22 and drive 10.0 miles to Dry Park, a large open meadow. The ride starts at the intersection of FR 22 and FR 226, which is also the starting point for Ride 21: Dry Park Lakes (see p. 110). FR 226, a minor dirt road, might not be signed.

To get to the ride's north end at Castle Canyon, drive south from Jacob Lake Inn on AZ 67 for 0.3 mile to FR 461. Turn right (west) on FR 461 and drive approximately 6.0 miles to FR 462. Go right (west). Drive about 3.0 miles on FR 462, then turn left (south) on FR 22. Go 7.0 miles on FR 22 to FR 429. Go left (east) on FR 429 for about 0.25 mile to FR 226. The trailhead is just south of FR 429 on FR 226.

Trail Overview
The Lookout Canyon Trail (Forest Service Trail #120) is a fun ride on a rarely used trail system. Summer wildflowers, fall colors, and wildlife sightings treat bikers as they pedal over excellent grade through alpine forest and meadows. The Lookout Canyon Trail is also a cool place to ride during the heat of summer.

The best way to ride this trail is to get dropped off at Dry Park and coast down to the trailhead at FR 429/FR 226. Intermediate cyclists who plan to ride out and back can bike down and up this trail in an enjoyable three hours. Beginners without a shuttle might want to start at the route's north end, then turn around and ride back down once they tire of climbing.

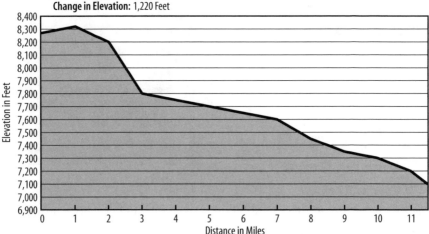

Ride 19 Total Elevation Gain: 50 Feet
Total Elevation Loss: 1,220 Feet
Change in Elevation: 1,220 Feet

Route Description

Mile

0.0/11.5 At the intersection of FR 22 and FR 226, go north following a double track that heads into a notchlike valley. This portion of the trail is closed to motorized vehicles until you reach mile 8.6.

0.3/11.2 Go past green gate poles and a powerline that follows the route for almost the entire way.

0.5/11.0 At the trail intersection, head left (west), following the sign that indicates the Lookout Canyon Trail. Make a quick climb into the forest.

1.0/10.5 Take a moment to appreciate the scenery as you enjoy a well-graded descent through a narrow canyon. Don't forget that if you are biking out and back, you'll have to ride back up.

2.2/9.3 A sign marks Trail #122. FR 22 is 1.2 miles to the southwest, but bicyclists might find the unimproved access trail to be difficult.

Mile

3.0/8.5   Lookout Canyon Tank might be dry during drought years.

6.0/5.5   A USFS sign says that FR 422 (the same road as FR 22) is 5.0 miles to the south. This spur trail, which looked overgrown when I was there, is Trail #121 at Pratt Canyon.

8.6/2.9   Go through a gate. Motorized traffic is allowed from here down to the trailhead at the ride's north end.

9.4/2.1   Pass through another gate. A stock tank in the corral has water.

9.8/1.7   A grassy campsite here makes a nice base camp for your vehicle support crew.

11.2/0.3   Check out the interesting rock formation on the side of the road. "Hoodoos" like this one are probably the reason this area is called Castle Canyon.

11.5/0.0   You arrive at the Lookout Canyon Trailhead parking area on FR 429. FR 22 is a short distance to the west.

A Forest Service sign points the way to Lookout Canyon.

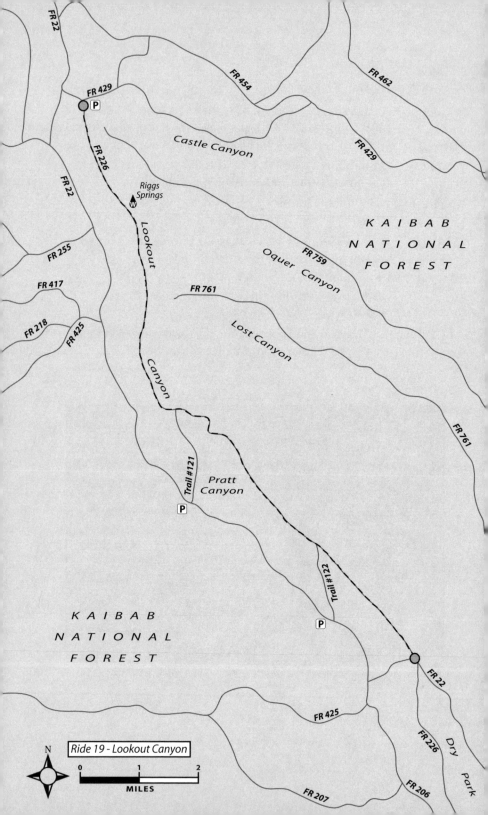

FR 22

FR 429
P

FR 454

FR 462

FR 429

Castle Canyon

FR 226

Riggs
Springs
W

FR 22

FR 255

Lookout

FR 417

FR 759

Oquer Canyon

K A I B A B

N A T I O N A L

F O R E S T

FR 761

FR 218

FR 425

Lost Canyon

Canyon

FR 761

Trail #121

Pratt
Canyon
P

Trail #122

P

K A I B A B

N A T I O N A L

F O R E S T

FR 22

FR 425

FR 226

Dry

Park

FR 206

Ride 19 - Lookout Canyon

N

0   1   2

MILES

FR 207

Ride 20 **THE BLOWDOWN**
See map, p. 109.

Distance: 7.0 miles

Difficulty: Moderate

Technical Rating:
Beginner

Type: Double-track/Road

Season
May to October.

Maps
USFS: North Kaibab
Ranger District

Signage
Poor: USFS markers on
Carsonite posts.

The meadows of the Kaibab Plateau are also known as mountain grassland parks.

Access to Trailhead
To access the ride's north end, go south from Jacob Lake Inn on AZ 67 for 26.5 miles to FR 22 at DeMotte Park. Go right (west) on FR 22 and drive for 8.7 miles to FR 422D, which is on the southeast side of the road just past the signed road that leads to the Dry Park Fire Tower. To start at the south end of the ride, drive south from Jacob Lake Inn on AZ 67 for 26.5 miles to FR 22. Go right (west) for 2.0 miles to FR 462. Go right (north) on FR 462 and continue for a short distance to FR 422D.

Trail Overview
This route borrows its name from an old blowdown area through which it travels. Quiet rides through alpine meadow and forest landscapes distinguish this rarely traveled portion of Lookout Canyon. Meadow wildflowers reward summer riders, whereas fall colors blow the mind in late September. You should expect some climbing in both directions, but because this route is mostly on a gradual grade, feel free to start at either end. This ride is unsigned, so map-reading skills are recommended.

Route Description

Mile

0.0/7.0   Park at the intersection of FR 22 and FR 422D. Take the dirt FR 422D southeast and descend under the powerline.

1.3/5.7   At the bottom of the hill, the track heads southeast through a meadow.

1.7/5.3   Continue through the meadow to a fork in the road. Take the left (southeast) fork and stay along the powerline. Ride through a narrow valley on a grassy double track.

4.4/2.6   The gradual grade rolls through an alley of evergreens that resemble Christmas trees.

5.0/2.0   The road ascends for 0.5 mile, then flattens out again. Pass the North Blowdown Tank, which might be dry during drought years. This is the area labeled as "The Blowdown" on topographic maps.

6.9/0.1   Go uphill and stay right (east) when you pass an old dirt track on the left.

7.0/0.0   FR 422D ends at FR 462. Turn around and enjoy the gradual descent until you reach the bottom of the hill and have to climb back to your vehicle at FR 22.

Ride 20   Total Elevation Gain: 550 Feet
Total Elevation Loss: 150 Feet
Change in Elevation: 550 Feet

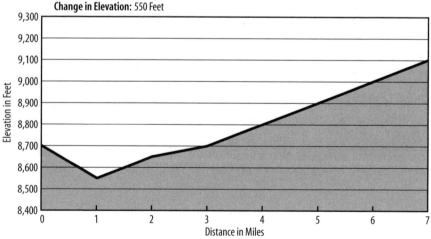

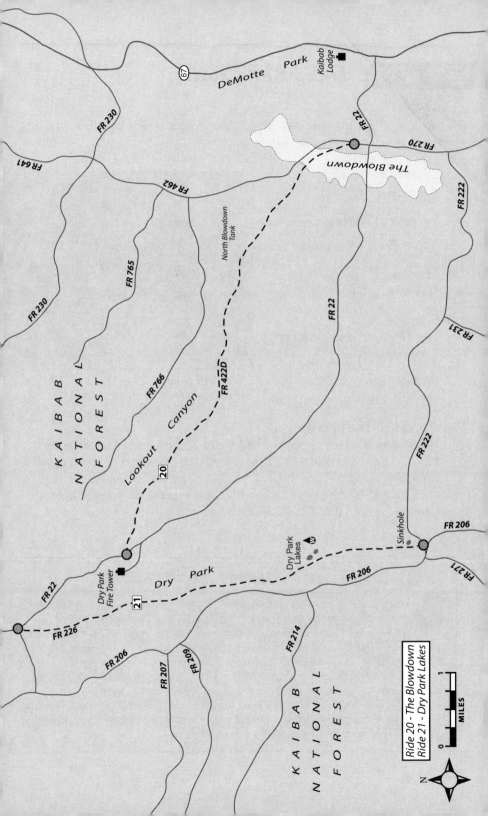

Ride 21 **DRY PARK LAKES**
See map, p. 109.

Kids who can handle geared bikes will love this nice, short ride.

Distance: 4.3 miles

Difficulty: Easy

Technical Rating: Beginner

Type: Double-track/Road

Season
May to October.

Signage
Fair: Forest road numbers on Carsonite posts.

Water Sources
Dry Park Lakes at mile 3.2.

Along with examples of sinkhole geology, grassy meadows dotted with strands of trees distinguish this ride.

Access to Trailhead
From Jacob Lake Inn, go south on AZ 67 for 26.5 miles to FR 22 at DeMotte Park. Go right (west) on FR 22 for about 10.0 miles and descend to an expansive meadow named Dry Park. The ride starts at the intersection of FR 22 and FR 226, which is also the starting point for Ride 19: Lookout Canyon (see p. 103). FR 226, a minor dirt road, might not be signed.

Lakes and Sinkholes of the Kaibab Plateau

Underneath the surface of the Kaibab Plateau is a porous layer of limestone that allows water to soak through. Because water rarely settles above ground, few permanent streams can form. The water instead creates caverns and tunnels that lie hidden below the surface. When these caverns collapse, they leave behind depressions called "sinkholes." Sometimes these sinkholes fill up with water and become what Arizonans call "lakes." Don't laugh. These stagnant ponds are an important source of water for wildlife as well as campers.

While biking across the meadows of Dry Park, you can see a good example of a dry sinkhole at mile 4.3 of this ride. The size of the trees growing in this large depression gives you some idea of how old this sinkhole might be.

Trail Overview

If any scenery could compete with the views from the rim of the Grand Canyon, it would be the meadows of the Kaibab Plateau. On this ride you roll through grassy fields dotted with spruce and fir, witnessing excellent examples of sinkhole geology along the way. This area works well as a base for car-camping. Morning riders have a good chance of spotting mule deer, elk, or wild turkeys, and coyotes might serenade campers at dusk. Dry Park Lakes is a good warm-up before you ride the Rainbow Rim Trail (see Ride 22, p. 112), and it makes a nice trip for beginners and families.

Route Description

Mile

0.0/4.3   From FR 22 at Dry Park, take the road marked FR 226 that heads south through a rolling meadow. The track is a little bumpy at first but gets better the farther south you go.

2.3/2.0   Take the track that bears right (west) and stay on the most improved road as it climbs slightly and enters a forest.

3.2/1.1   The Dry Park Lakes are sinkholes that have filled with water. There should be a nice pond behind the corral.

3.7/0.6   Pass by several grassy campsites.

4.3/0.0   Check out the sinkhole on the left (east) side of the road. You can turn around here or ride just a little farther to the intersection with FR 222.

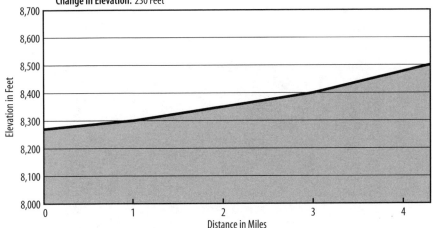

Ride 21 Total Elevation Gain: 230 Feet
Total Elevation Loss: 0 Feet
Change in Elevation: 230 Feet

Ride 22 ▸ ***RAINBOW RIM TRAIL***
See map, p. 115.

 ***Older teen-agers who can handle geared bikes should
have fun riding at least part of this trail.***

Distance: 18.4 miles

Difficulty: Moderate

Technical Rating: Intermediate

Type: Single-track/Trail

Season
May to October, but perhaps a longer timeframe depending on the
onset and severity of the snow season.

Signage
Good: Wooden signs and Carsonite posts.

Access to Trailhead
From Jacob Lake Inn, drive south on AZ 67 for 26.5 miles to FR 22 at
DeMotte Park. Go right (west) on FR 22 for 10.5 miles to FR 206. Take
FR 206 left (south) to the road leading to your desired starting point.
The roads are well signed. For Parissawampitts Point at the end of this
ride, take FR 214. For Fence Point, take FR 293. For Locust Point, take
FR 294. For North Timp Point, take FR 271 to FR 271A and go right
(north, then west). To reach Timp Point, where this trail description
begins, take FR 271 all the way to the end.

*Rim-skirting views and fun single track make the Rainbow Rim
Trail a classic Arizona Ride.*

Trail Overview

The Rainbow Rim Trail travels along the edge of the Grand Canyon for 18.4 spectacular miles. The single-track trail stays within 5 to 300 feet of the rim and has no major climbs. Some have described the Rainbow Rim Trail as the best single track in the Four Corners area. You won't experience the crowds you see in Moab, Utah, even though you might encounter a few commercial bike tour groups.

Although experienced and well-conditioned mountain bikers can ride the entire trail out and back in a day, most will want to split the ride in half. This trail is fun, fun, fun! Why rush it? Primitive camping sites are plentiful at several points along the route, the best sites with views being at Timp, North Timp, and Locust. Nearly halfway through the ride, Locust Point serves as an excellent base camp for those wanting to spend two days riding the trail.

Route Description

Mile

0.0/18.4   Take the signed trail from the trailhead parking area at Timp Point/FR 271.

0.9/17.5   Enjoy a nice downhill, then a moderate climb. Roll over some hard, smooth single track.

3.0/15.4   Get out the camera for some action shots at this fine vista at North Timp Trailhead/FR 271A. From here, the trail continues north along the rim over similar terrain.

6.5/11.9   Descend to a meadow, and then make a short but tough climb.

7.1/11.3   Top out on the climb.

8.7/9.7   The trail travels alongside FR 294 and by several campsites with views.

9.3/9.1   Locust Point/FR 294 has plenty of sites for car-camping and several short trails to overlooks. You can turn around at this midpoint for a shorter day ride, or if you prefer to continue on from Locust Point Trailhead, go down to a meadow then up a gradual 0.5-mile climb. Pass several scenic meadows and canyon views.

11.7/6.7   Pay attention. Don't let the views distract you too much as the trail skirts the rim of the canyon for the next mile.

12.4/6.0   Here is Fence Point/FR 293.

Mile

14.7/3.7   Enjoy a long, fun descent to a meadow, then grunt up another long but well-graded climb.

16.1/2.3   The worst is over. Now cruise the winding single track through the meadows.

17.9/0.5   More views open up as the trail again skirts the edge of the canyon.

18.4/0.0   Make a steep climb up a hill to reach the parking area at Parissawampitts Point.

Loop   *This trail is fun enough to warrant an out-and-back ride, but if you're itching for a loop, you can take FR 214 east from Parissawampitts Point for 3.6 miles to FR 250. Go right (south) on FR 250 back to the road that leads to the trailhead where you started. FR 250 has several steep climbs out of drainages, so this loop doesn't save you much more time than just taking the trail back. If you ride this loop to the end at Timp Point, the trip measures 30.5 miles. Well-conditioned cyclists could complete the entire circuit in five hours. Take plenty of water.*

Ride 22   Total Elevation Gain: 600 Feet
Total Elevation Loss: 700 Feet
Change in Elevation: 250 Feet

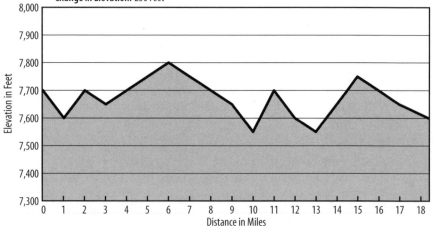

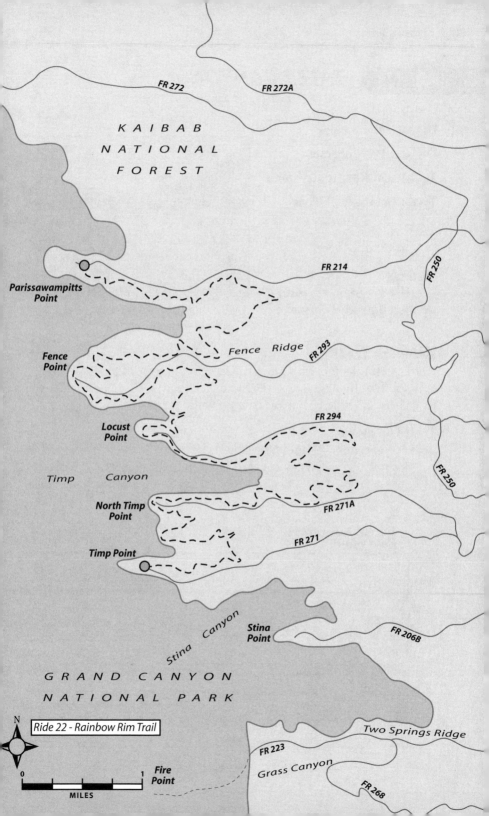

FR 272   FR 272A

K A I B A B
N A T I O N A L
F O R E S T

FR 214

FR 250

Parissawampitts
Point

Fence   Ridge   FR 293

Fence
Point

FR 294

Locust
Point

FR 250

Timp   Canyon

North Timp
Point

FR 271A

Timp Point

FR 271

Stina   Canyon   Stina
Point   FR 206B

G R A N D   C A N Y O N
N A T I O N A L   P A R K

N

Ride 22 - Rainbow Rim Trail

Two Springs Ridge

0   1

MILES

Fire
Point

FR 223   Grass Canyon

FR 268

Ride 23 **TATER CANYON**
See map, p. 125.

Distance: 4.8 miles

Difficulty: Moderate

Technical Rating: Beginner

Type: Double-track/Road

Season
May to October.

Signage
Fair: USFS road numbers on
wooden signs and Carsonite
posts.

*Look for turkeys and elk when you ride in Tater
Canyon in the early morning.*

Access to Trailhead
From Jacob Lake Inn, go south on AZ 67 for 27.5 miles to FR 611 (0.6
mile south of the entrance to DeMotte Campground). Go left (east) on
FR 611 for 0.3 mile to the intersection with FR 424A.

Trail Overview
With the exception of a tough climb and descent at the beginning, this
is a nice ride that follows an old road through the meadows at the bottom
of Tater Canyon. This route also offers access to the Arizona Trail (AZT)

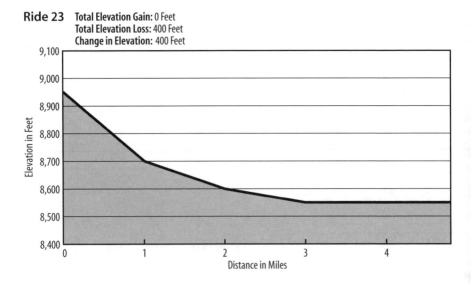

Ride 23   **Total Elevation Gain:** 0 Feet
Total Elevation Loss: 400 Feet
Change in Elevation: 400 Feet

and the potential to make circuit rides of varying distances by connecting the AZT and other Forest Service roads. Wildlife sightings are likely for early morning riders.

Route Description

Mile

0.0/4.8	Take FR 424A northeast from where it intersects with FR 611 and begin climbing.
0.2/4.6	Go left (west) near the top of the climb, then descend for 1.0 mile into a meadow valley.
1.2/3.6	You are now in Upper Tater Canyon. Enjoy a gradual grade, although the road might get sandy at times. In the summer months, look for purple lupine blooming under the pines.
2.0/2.8	Pass by the remains of an old corral.
2.5/2.3	Several roads come in from the west. Stay right (east) on the road leading up the valley's main drainage.
3.5/1.3	At the AZT sign, this route joins with the AZT and follows the road north for the remainder of the ride. From here, intermediate bikers could ride the AZT south toward East Rim View and then take either FR 610 or FR 611 back to the ride's start.
4.8/0.0	The AZT leaves the road and turns into single track as it enters the forest. Turn around here or stay on the AZT for a while longer if you aren't getting enough of the sights.

Talking Turkey

Sometime after 1946, wild turkeys from southern Arizona were introduced on the Kaibab Plateau. The species thrived. Today, flocks of wild turkeys often appear in the meadows of the North Rim during the morning hours.

Wild turkeys also live deep in the Grand Canyon. If you can find a bottle of Phantom Ranch Amber Ale, look for a turkey in the photograph on the label. This is Kathy. Kathy the turkey decided to make the grounds at Phantom Ranch her home, so she became a favorite of park rangers and visitors at the canyon-bottom destination. Although rangers believe that Kathy has since died, sightings of other turkeys living inside the Grand Canyon have been reported.

Ride 24 ▶ FALL COLOR LOOP

See map, p. 125.

Distance: 15.3 miles

Difficulty: Moderate

Technical Rating:
Intermediate

Type: Single-track/Trail and
Double-track/Road

Season
May to October.

Signage
Good: AZT stickers on
Carsonite posts.

Water Sources
At mile 10.4, Crystal Spring is
contained in a small concrete
tank behind a wooden fence.

Access to Trailhead
From Jacob Lake Inn, drive
27.5 miles south on AZ 67
to FR 611, 0.6 mile past the

A short, paved path links FR 611 to the overlook at East Rim View.

entrance to DeMotte Campground. Turn left (east) on FR 611 and go
1.4 miles to FR 610. Go right (south) on FR 610 for 5.0 miles to the
Boundary Trailhead of the Arizona Trail (AZT). There is a parking lot
with a restroom but no water.

Trail Overview
I was lucky enough to ride this route during the peak of the fall color
season, hence the name. However, if your timing is off, the views of the
east side of the Grand Canyon and a sampling of some of the best single
track found on the Arizona Trail should fend off any disappointment. The
overall grade is slightly better if you ride this loop in a counter-clockwise
direction from the Boundary Trailhead. The single-track portion does
involve a few climbs that all but the fittest and most experienced mountain
bikers will find tough. The alpine scenery in this area is stunning, however.
So, if you are a beginner, don't let a little bike-pushing get in the way of
experiencing some of the best sights the Arizona Trail has to offer.

Route Description

Mile

0.0/15.3 From the AZT's Boundary Trailhead, go left (west) on FR 610. This gravel road rolls up and down at first, then mostly descends.

5.0/10.3 At the four-way intersection, go right (east, then north) on FR 611. The road climbs for the most part, but the grade is easy to handle.

8.0/7.3 At the East Rim View Trailhead, go right (east) onto the paved path to the overlook. After checking out the view of the Saddle Mountain Wilderness, take the AZT to the right (south).

8.9/6.4 The single track winds through a forest along the edge of the East Rim.

9.1/6.2 As you drop off the East Rim, the trail gets loose, rocky, and steep.

10.4/4.9 Crystal Spring, an excellent water source, is contained in a small concrete tank behind a wooden fence. Remember to treat the water before drinking it, and camp at least 100 yards away.

11.3/4.0 The trail leaves a faint road and jumps onto single track. Ascend a steep section through a forest of aspen mixed with evergreens the size of Christmas trees.

Ride 24 Total Elevation Gain: 430 Feet
Total Elevation Loss: 430 Feet
Change in Elevation: 400 Feet

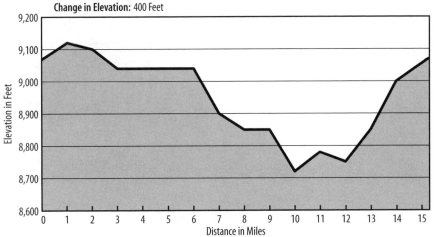

Mile

11.7/3.6   Cross a gravel road, then in 0.2 mile cross a dirt road marked only with a rock cairn. Stay on the single track as you pass through a series of beautiful meadows.

12.1/3.2   As you leave the meadowlands, get ready for two steep ascents through stands of large, white-barked aspen.

13.0/2.3   You might find some water in the sinkholes just south of Sourdough Well (the well is covered with a concrete cap). When you see a road coming in, stay on the well-marked single track that travels through a long, narrow meadow.

13.9/1.4   Continue a gradual ascent up a canyon on a well-defined trail.

15.0/0.3   After you cross FR 610, look for a signed trail heading up to your right (northwest) to the Boundary Trailhead.

15.3/0.0   Return to the Boundary Trailhead parking lot.

The Arizona Trail

Thanks to the inspiration of a Flagstaff schoolteacher named Dale Shewalter, the state of Arizona has its very own long-distance trail. Stretching nearly 800 miles from Utah to Mexico, the Arizona Trail (AZT) traverses seven mountain ranges, crosses four rivers, passes by five lakes, and visits three national parks and four national forests. Outdoor enthusiasts can explore the trail by foot, bike, or horseback. The AZT starts at the Utah border and travels across the Kaibab Plateau to the rim of the Grand Canyon at the North Kaibab Trailhead. Along with this bike ride, several of the other routes described in this book give you a taste of the adventure the AZT has to offer: the Multi-Use Trail (see Ride 16, p. 94) and Crystal Spring (see Ride 25, p. 122) on the North Rim, and the Coconino Rim Loop (see Ride 14, p. 82) on the South Rim.

The AZT follows the Kaibab Plateau Trail as it travels through the Kaibab National Forest.

Hardy mountain bikers can ride The Arizona Trail from Utah to Mexico.

Ride 25 ▶ CRYSTAL SPRING

See map, p. 125.

Older kids might enjoy trying this single track. For an easier ride, you can turn around at mile 2.3 at Sourdough Well.

Distance: 4.9 miles

Difficulty: Moderate

Technical Rating: Beginner

Type: Single-track/Trail

Season
May to October.

Signage
Good: AZT stickers on Carsonite posts.

Water Sources
At the end of the ride, Crystal Spring is contained in a small concrete tank behind a wooden fence.

Riders on the trail to Crystal Spring pedal their way through some of the Kaibab Plateau's loveliest meadows.

Access to Trailhead

From Jacob Lake Inn, drive 27.5 miles south on AZ 67 to FR 611, 0.6 mile past the entrance to DeMotte Campground. Turn left (east) on FR 611 and go 1.4 miles to FR 610. Go right (south) on FR 610 for 5.0 miles to the Boundary Trailhead of the Arizona Trail (AZT). There is a parking lot with a restroom but no water.

Trail Overview

The trail to Crystal Spring takes you on a fantastic ride that samples some of the Kaibab Plateau's prettiest meadows, where you might witness wildlife and stunning fall color displays. At the time of printing, the portion of the AZT south of the Boundary Trailhead remained incomplete; however, you may ride a short distance south of the National Park Service boundary if you'd like. As soon as the NPS completes the trail, you will be able to ride south from the Boundary Trailhead all the way into the park.

Ride 25   Total Elevation Gain: 100 Feet
Total Elevation Loss: 390 Feet
Change in Elevation: 320 Feet

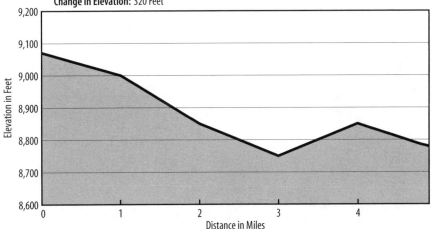

Route Description

Mile

0.0/4.9   From the Boundary Trailhead on FR 610, take the signed access spur to the AZT. At the first intersection, take the right (northeast) fork of the AZT toward Sourdough Well. You are now heading northbound on the AZT and will cross FR 610 very soon.

Mile

0.3/4.6	After crossing the gravel road, follow the single-track trail that heads northwest through the meadow.
1.4/3.5	Make a gradual descent on a well-defined trail.
2.3/2.6	The single track travels through a long meadow and passes Sourdough Well, which is covered with a concrete cap. You might find some water in the sinkholes just south of Sourdough Well.
3.2/1.7	Make two steep descents through forests of white-barked aspen trees, then enjoy a series of scenic alpine meadows.
3.6/1.3	Cross a dirt road marked only with a rock cairn, then cross a gravel road in another 0.2 mile.
4.0/0.9	Make another descent through a forest of Christmas-tree-size evergreens, before the trail joins a faint road.
4.9/0.0	Crystal Spring is contained in a small concrete tank behind a wooden fence. This is an excellent source of clear natural water (make sure to treat it before drinking it). It also makes a great place to enjoy lunch before you turn around and start the climbs back to the trailhead.

Be sure to make hunters aware of your presence when you're riding through national forest areas during autumn.

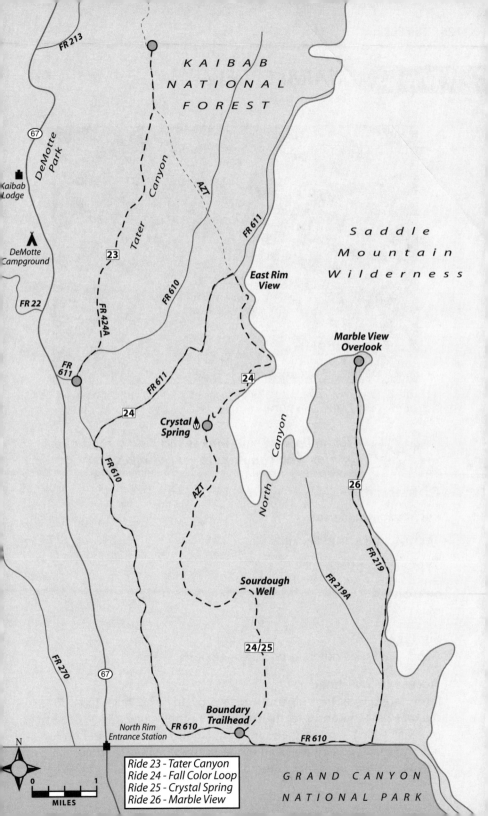

FR 213

KAIBAB
NATIONAL
FOREST

67

DeMotte
Park

Kaibab
Lodge

DeMotte
Campground

FR 22

Tater Canyon

AZT

23

FR 610

FR 424A

FR 611

East Rim
View

FR 611

Saddle
Mountain
Wilderness

Marble View
Overlook

FR 611

24

FR 610

24

Crystal
Spring

AZT

North Canyon

26

FR 219

FR 219A

Sourdough
Well

24/25

FR 270

67

North Rim
Entrance Station

FR 610

Boundary
Trailhead

FR 610

N

GRAND CANYON
NATIONAL PARK

Ride 23 - Tater Canyon
Ride 24 - Fall Color Loop
Ride 25 - Crystal Spring
Ride 26 - Marble View

0   1
MILES

Ride 26 MARBLE VIEW

See map, p. 125.

The dirt road ride to Marble View Overlook ends with breathtaking views of the Saddle Mountain Wilderness and the Grand Canyon's east side.

 The mellow terrain makes this ride a good one for kids who can handle geared bikes.

Distance: 6.8 miles

Difficulty: Moderate

Technical Rating: Beginner

Type: Double-track/Road

Season
May to October.

Signage
Good: USFS road numbers on Carsonite posts.

Access to Trailhead
From Jacob Lake Inn, go south on AZ 67 for 27.5 miles to FR 611, 0.6 mile past the entrance to DeMotte Campground. Go left (east) on FR 611 for 1.4 miles, then turn right (south) on FR 610 and go 5.0 miles to the Boundary Trailhead of the Arizona Trail (AZT). There is a parking lot with a restroom but no water.

Trail Overview

This dirt road ride culminates in an outstanding view of the east side of the Grand Canyon. From Marble View Overlook you can see Marble Canyon, Navajo Mountain, the Vermilion Cliffs, and the Saddle Mountain Wilderness. You might spot red-tailed hawks taking advantage of the thermal air currents that rise from the canyon.

Route Description

Mile

0.0/6.8   From the AZT's Boundary Trailhead parking area, head east on FR 610. The road parallels the NPS boundary as it rolls through a forest of aspen and fir.

2.0/4.8   At the intersection, turn left (north) onto FR 219. Begin a gradual climb.

2.7/4.1   At the intersection with FR 219A, stay right (east) on FR 219. The road flattens out as it travels through an alley of aspen for the next 3.0 miles. Fall colors in this area are amazing.

5.0/1.8   Some topo maps show Marble Sinkhole off to the right, east of where the road bends to the northeast. I missed it when I was there, but it looks like it might be worth checking out.

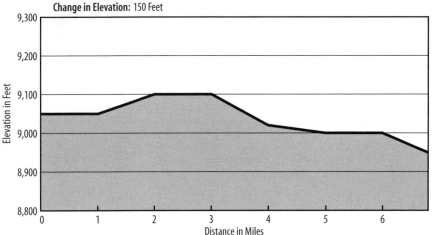

Ride 26   Total Elevation Gain: 50 Feet
Total Elevation Loss: 150 Feet
Change in Elevation: 150 Feet

Mile

6.8/0.0   There are two overlooks here at the turnaround point. Continue right (east) through the trees to an expansive view of the east side of the Grand Canyon. At the bottom of the ridge, directly below the main overlook, notice the outcroppings of beige and red rocks called the Cocks Combs.

Avoid the crowds at the Grand Canyon by venturing out to Marble View Overlook, where you can catch a unique look at the canyon's east side.

Ride 27 ▸ *JUMPUP POINT*

See map, p. 132.

Distance: 7.8 miles

Difficulty: Strenuous

Technical Rating: Intermediate

Type: Double-track/Road

Season
Late spring to late fall, but winter riding might be an option during years of little snowfall.

Maps
USFS: Kaibab National Forest, North Kaibab Ranger District

Signage
Fair: USFS road numbers on Carsonite posts.

Situated at the end of a narrow peninsula, Jumpup Point overlooks a spectacular and rarely seen portion of the Grand Canyon.

Access to Trailhead
From downtown Fredonia, go south on US 89A. Look for the turnoff for FR 22 (paved at first) about 2.0 miles south of town. Take FR 22 south for about 23.0 miles to the intersection with FR 423. Turn right (west) on FR 423. From here, follow the directions in the last paragraph of this section, starting at the FR 22/FR 423 intersection.

From Jacob Lake Inn, go south on AZ 67 for 0.3 mile to FR 461. Turn right (west) onto FR 461 and go 5.5 miles to FR 462. Turn right (west) on FR 462 and drive 3.0 miles to FR 22. Take FR 22 left (south) for 2.0 miles to FR 423. From here, follow the directions below.

From the intersection of FR 22 and FR 423 outside of area shown (see North Rim Overview map, p. 92), go southwest for 3.0 miles on FR 423 to FR 235. Go right (north, then west) on FR 235 for 8.0 miles to where it reconnects with FR 423. Now go right (southwest) on FR 423 for 4.5 miles to the intersection with FR 201 at Jumpup Divide. You can start here, but I recommend that you drive 2.5 miles south on FR 201 to the intersection with the primitive FR 649. The trail description begins at the FR 201/FR 649 intersection.

Trail Overview

If you ride the entire route out to Jumpup Point, you'll have to grind your way up several steep climbs as the road rolls over a narrow peninsula between the deep canyons of the Kanab Creek Wilderness. Near the end, the riding gets easier and the scenery gets better. Therefore, beginners with high-clearance vehicles might want to drive out to the point, ride the easier spur roads found at the terminus of FR 201, and then make their way up the peninsula from its end.

The views at Jumpup Point are spectacular and camping at the overlook is an outstanding experience in a remote, rarely seen area of the Grand Canyon. The entire route is exposed to the sun, so bring the sunscreen. Because of the area's isolation, be sure to take plenty of water and supplies, too.

Route Description

Mile

0.0/7.8   Park at the intersection of FR 201 and FR 649, then go south on FR 201. The road starts out with a rolling grade through piñon-juniper forest with occasional views to the north and southwest.

0.6/7.2   The road skirts the edge of Jumpup Canyon through a skeleton forest of burnt juniper. Expect a few steep hills that are short enough to not pose too much of a challenge.

1.9/5.9   Stay on the main road (FR 201) along the east edge of the peninsula.

2.5/5.3   The hills get steeper, longer, and higher.

4.4/3.4   Stay east (left) on FR 201 at the intersection with FR 651. FR 651 might make an interesting spur ride for those camping at the overlook.

4.7/3.1   Here is a decent view into Jumpup Canyon. The twisting channel of the canyon below is known as The Gooseneck.

5.5/2.3   There are more hills to climb, but the views become worth the effort.

6.9/0.9   The grade eases up a bit for the last mile.

7.8/0.0   At the end, you can stop and enjoy your hard-earned view or continue for an easy 0.6 mile to another, less scenic overlook to the west. The smooth, reddish layer of stone you see below is called the Esplanade, part of the Supai Formation. You can see Mount Trumbull and Mount Logan to the west. To the southeast is the main canyon formed by the Colorado River.

Ride 27 Total Elevation Gain: 150 Feet
Total Elevation Loss: 250 Feet
Change in Elevation: 200 Feet

The scenic solitude of Jumup Point makes it an ideal destination for a camping trip.

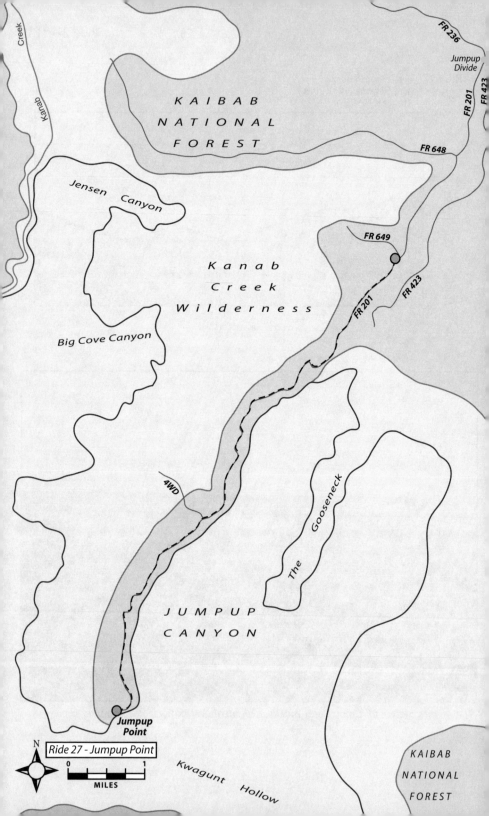

Creek

Kanab

Jensen Canyon

KAIBAB

NATIONAL

FOREST

FR 236

Jumpup
Divide

FR 201

FR 423

FR 648

FR 649

FR 201

FR 423

K a n a b

C r e e k

W i l d e r n e s s

Big Cove Canyon

4WD

The Gooseneck

J U M P U P

C A N Y O N

Jumpup
Point

Ride 27 - Jumpup Point

N

0   1

MILES

Kwagunt   Hollow

KAIBAB

NATIONAL

FOREST

Appendix A **RIDES for the LONG-DISTANCE BIKER**

I am a long-distance thru-biker at heart. I like to load my bike down with all the gear, food, and water I need so that I can spend several days getting an intimate feel for a place. Therefore, I have listed a few routes that make fine long-distance rides for experienced mountain bikers or those who want to try a multiday bikepacking tour.

SOUTH RIM

The Rock and Road

For a longer day ride that offers a nice combination of trail- and road-riding, start at the Tusayan Bike Trails Trailhead (see Ride 1, p. 38), and ride Loop 3. At mile 5.7 on Loop 3, go east on Trail #4, a mostly single-track trail through ponderosa forests, to the trailhead at Grandview Lookout—a total of 16.4 miles one way from the Tusayan Bike Trails Trailhead. From Grandview Lookout, ride north on FR 310 to AZ 64. Turn left (west) onto the paved AZ 64 and take it all the way back to the Tusayan Bike Trails Trailhead for a 35-mile loop. Experienced mountain bikers can do this loop in one day.

South Rim Village to Pasture Wash

This long road leads to a historic and dilapidated ranger station. The scenery gets a bit monotonous as you travel across sagebrush plains, but hardcore long-distance bikers might want to take on this 23-mile ride (one way). You can camp out near the ranger station (no facilities, no water), but first obtain a permit from the NPS Backcountry Information Center (see Appendix C). You can also get more detailed directions from the rangers at the backcountry office. The road to Pasture Wash crosses land owned by the Havasupai tribe. Be prepared to pay a $20 fee to enter the reservation.

To do this ride, start from the Moqui Lodge just north of Tusayan and follow the directions for The Backdoor (see Ride 9, p. 67). Follow these directions to mile 5.0, where you exit The Backdoor route by staying on FR 328 and heading west. Follow the signs to Pasture Wash. You will pass by several stock tanks that might have water, but don't count on it. This route is for experienced and self-reliant mountain bikers. Wet weather or snow might render the road impassable.

Grandview Lookout to Buffalo Park (Flagstaff) via the Arizona Trail

For detailed information about this premier bike route, which follows the historic Moqui Stagecoach Route for 86.0 miles one way, see my other book, *Biking the Arizona Trail: The Complete Guide to Day-Riding and Thru-Biking.*

NORTH RIM
Toughing It Out to Tuweep

Also known as Toroweap, Tuweep is a secluded area at the Grand Canyon's northwest rim. A long, dusty stretch of dirt road leads to the Toroweap Overlook, where you can admire one of the most impressive—and most isolated—views of the Grand Canyon. At the overlook, the canyon drops a dramatic 3,000 vertical feet to the Colorado River.

To ride this route, drive west from Fredonia, Arizona, on AZ 389 for about 7.0 miles to BLM Road 109. Start your ride by going south from the intersection of AZ 389 and BLM 109, staying on the most traveled dirt/gravel road and following the signs to the Tuweep Ranger Station. After a rugged and remote 61.0 miles, you reach the end of the line, where a primitive, first-come, first-served campground sits near the rim. Tuweep offers no food, water, or services, but a park ranger is stationed in this area year-round. Bikers should plan on taking at least three days to do the entire 122-mile route, out and back. This is a ride for experienced, self-reliant thru-bikers or for those with vehicle support. BLM 109 might be impassable after heavy rains.

Utah State Line to North Kaibab Trailhead via the Arizona Trail

My book *Biking the Arizona Trail* also gives you all the information you need to complete this classic Arizona Trail ride to the Grand Canyon, perhaps the most scenic 68.5 miles you will ever bike.

Appendix B ▶ BIKE SHOPS, OUTFITTERS, and GUIDE SERVICES

Bike Shops (Rentals, Repairs, and Gear)

Flagstaff, Arizona
Absolute Bikes, 18 N. San Francisco St. (downtown), (928) 779-5969
Cosmic Cycles, 901 N. Beaver St. (downtown), (928) 779-1092
Loose Spoke, 1529 S. Milton Rd., (928) 774-7428
Mountain Sports, 1800 S. Milton Rd., Suite 100, (928) 779-5156
Sinagua Cycles, 113 S. San Francisco St. (downtown), (928) 779-9969
Single Track Bikes, 575 Riordan Rd., (928) 773-1862

Page, Arizona
Red Rock Cyclery, 819 N. Navajo Dr., (520) 645-1479

St. George, Utah
Bicycles Unlimited, 90 South 100 East, (888) 673-4492
Red Rock Bicycle, 190 S. Main St., (435) 674-3185

Outfitters (Camping and Recreation Gear)

Grand Canyon National Park
Babbitt's General Store, South Rim (next to the post office), (928) 638-2854

Flagstaff, Arizona
Aspen Sports, 15 N. San Francisco St. (downtown), (928) 779-1935
Babbitt's Backcountry Outfitters, 12 E. Aspen Ave. (downtown), (928) 774-4775
Peace Surplus, 14 W. Route 66 (downtown), (928) 779-4521

St. George, Utah
Outdoor Outlet, 1062 E. Tabernacle, (800) 726-8106

Guide Services (Bike Trips at the Grand Canyon)

Arizona Outback Adventures/Wheels 'n' Gear, (866) 455-1601,
    www.azoutbackadventures.com
Arizona White-Knuckle Adventures, (866) 342-9669,
    www.arizona-adventures.com (good for a family bonding trip)
Canyon Rim Adventures, (800) 897-9633, www.canyonrimadventures.com
High Sonoran Adventures, (877) GRAND-11, www.bikethecanyon.com
    (offers a family camping trip)
Rim Tours, (800) 626-7335, www.rimtours.com
Western Spirit, (800) 845-2453, www.westernspirit.com
    (good for a South Rim family trip)

Appendix C ▶ AGENCIES and ORGANIZATIONS

National Park Service: Grand Canyon National Park
Backcountry Information Center
P.O. Box 129
Grand Canyon, AZ 86023
(928) 638-7875
www.nps.gov/grca/backcountry/

United States Forest Service: Kaibab National Forest
North Kaibab Ranger District
430 S. Main
Fredonia, AZ 86022
(928) 643-7395
www.fs.fed.us/r3/kai/

Tusayan Ranger District
P.O. Box 3088
Grand Canyon, AZ 86023
(928) 638-2443
www.fs.fed.us/r3/kai/

Bicycling Organizations

Adventure Cycling Association
P.O. Box 8308
Missoula, MT 59807
(800) 755-2453
www.adventurecycling.org

International Mountain Bicycling Association (IMBA)
1121 Broadway, Suite 203
P.O. Box 7578
Boulder, CO 80306
(888) 442-4622
www.imba.com

League of American Bicyclists
1612 K St. NW, Suite 800
Washington, DC 20006
(202) 822-1333
www.bikeleague.org

Mountain Biking Association of Arizona (MBAA)
P.O. Box 32728
Phoenix, AZ 85064
(602) 351-7430
www.mbaa.net

Arizona Trail Association
P.O. Box 36736
Phoenix, AZ 85067
(602) 252-4794
www.aztrail.org

Appendix D ▶ REFERENCES and SUGGESTED READING

Grand Canyon Natural and Cultural History

Anderson, Michael F. *Living at the Edge: Explorers, Exploiters and Settlers of the Grand Canyon Region.* Grand Canyon, Ariz.: Grand Canyon Association, 1998.

Annerino, John. *Hiking the Grand Canyon.* San Francisco: Sierra Club Books, 1993.

Coder, Christopher M. *An Introduction to Grand Canyon Prehistory.* Grand Canyon, Ariz.: Grand Canyon Association, 2000.

Ghiglieri, Michael P., and Thomas M. Myers. *Over the Edge: Death in Grand Canyon.* Flagstaff, Ariz.: Puma Press, 2001.

Grand Canyon National Park. *The Guide.* Grand Canyon, Ariz.: Grand Canyon Association, 2002.

Hughes, J. Donald. *In the House of Stone and Light: A Human History of the Grand Canyon.* Grand Canyon, Ariz.: Grand Canyon Association, 1978.

Loving, Nancy J. *Along the Rim: A Road Guide to the South Rim of Grand Canyon.* Grand Canyon, Ariz.: Grand Canyon Association, 1981.

Mangum, Richard K., and Sherry G. Mangum. *Grand Canyon–Flagstaff Stage Coach Line: A History & Exploration Guide.* Flagstaff, Ariz.: Hexagon Press, 1999.

Mauer, Stephen, ed. *Kaibab National Forest Visitors Guide: Williams, Chandler, and Tusayan Ranger Districts.* Albuquerque, N.M.: Southwest Natural and Cultural Heritage Association, 1990.

Pyne, Stephen J. *How the Canyon Became Grand: A Short History.* New York: Penguin Putnam, 1999.

Schmidt, Jeremy. *Grand Canyon National Park: A Natural History Guide.* New York: Houghton Mifflin Company, 1993.

United States Forest Service. *Historic Routes and Sites.* Tusayan, Ariz.: Kaibab National Forest, Tusayan Ranger District.

Whitney, Stephen R. *A Field Guide to the Grand Canyon.* Seattle: The Mountaineers Books, 1996.

Bicycle Maintenance and Touring

Adventure Cyclist Magazine. Missoula, Mont.: Adventure Cycling Association.

Grove, Eric, and Ron Cordes. *Pocket Guide to Emergency Bicycle Repair.* Helena, Mont.: Troutbeck/Greycliff, 1999.

Lankford, Andrea. *Biking the Arizona Trail: The Complete Guide to Day-Riding and Thru-Biking.* Englewood, Colo.: Westcliffe Publishers, 2002.

Lovett, Richard A. *The Essential Touring Cyclist: A Complete Guide for the Bicycle Traveler.* Camden, Maine: Ragged Mountain Press/McGraw Hill Publishing, 1994.

McCoy, Michael. *Cycling the Great Divide: From Canada to Mexico on America's Premier Long-Distance Mountain Bike Route.* Seattle: The Mountaineers Books, 2000.

Ray, Cosmic. *Fat Tire Tales and Trails: Arizona Mountain Bike Trail Guide.* Flagstaff, Ariz.: Cosmic Ray/New Millennium, 2000.

Bicycling with Children

Bell, Trudy E. *Bicycling with Children: A Complete How-To Guide.* Seattle: The Mountaineers Books, 1999.

Doan, Marlyn. *The Sierra Club Family Outdoors Guide: Hiking, Backpacking, Camping, Bicycling, Water Sports, and Winter Activities with Children.* San Francisco: Sierra Club Books, 1995.

Ross, Cindy, and Todd Gladfelter. *Kids in the Wild: A Family Guide to Outdoor Recreation.* Seattle: The Mountaineers Books, 1995.

Wilderness Medicine

Forgey, William W., M.D. *Wilderness Medicine: Beyond First Aid.* Guilford, Conn.: Globe Pequot Press, 1999.

Tilton, Buck, and Frank Hubbell. *Medicine for the Backcountry: A Practical Guide to Wilderness First Aid.* Guilford, Conn.: Globe Pequot Press, 1999.

Index

About the Author

After earning a bachelor's degree in forestry from the University of Tennessee, **Andrea Lankford** became a park ranger for the National Park Service. For 12 years, Andrea practiced emergency medicine, law enforcement, and search and rescue in several national parks including Zion, Yosemite, and the Grand Canyon. In 1999, Andrea left the park service and began to travel. Since then, she has hiked, biked, and kayaked more than 6,000 miles. Her journeys include a thru-hike of the Appalachian Trail, paddling the length of the Florida Keys from Miami to Key West, and cycling 414 miles to the Arctic Ocean along Alaska's Dalton Highway. In 2000, she and a fellow adventurer, Beth Overton, became the first to

mountain bike the length of the Arizona Trail. The resulting book, *Biking the Arizona Trail: The Complete Guide to Day-Riding and Thru-Biking* (Westcliffe Publishers, 2002), was Andrea's first. Stories from her adventures have appeared in several magazines including *Backpacker*, *Paddler*, and *Adventure Cyclist*. She currently lives in Los Angeles with her husband, Kent Delbon, and their bulldog, Shiloh.